THE NEW AMERICAN
DREAMER

How to Land That Ideal Job in a
Nightmare Economy

BY JASON VEDUCCIO

WAT AGE Publishing, LLC
www.wat-agepublishing.com
917-584-2931

Cover design by Kathryn Davenel

ISBN: 0615980694
ISBN 13: 9780615980690

To Audrey
My Grandmother And Friend

TABLE OF CONTENTS

MAKING YOUR DREAMS A REALITY
THE NEW AMERICAN DREAMER

Change happens slowly in spurts and fits, and as you read this book you do so sitting on the precipice of a new age. We are now entering a time when a whole generation will only know a digital existence, when dwindling resources have caused every person on the planet to conserve and re-utilize, and when economic and creative opportunities have exploded but only for those prepared with the right skill set and know-how.

However, you picked this book up for practical purposes, not big picture-speak, right? You might be sitting on the train reading this on your device, sitting in a coffee shop looking through job postings, or flipping screens back and forth between this article and that Excel spreadsheet due tomorrow morning.

Wherever you are in your career you need to be in a constant state of growing, even if you wish to simply keep the status quo. Why you ask? Because the new status quo is 'on the go'. As more markets emerge worldwide one must grow to maintain, and to advance one must innovate. So perpetual learning has now become something necessary to compete. Not a bad thing, right?

But you have to pick up the children from practice and you need to work late and you need to go to a meeting and who in their right mind has time to learn? This book shouldn't be pulling you away from yoga; to the contrary it should eventually allow you more time for your life by giving you freedom.

The New American Dream is not tied to a home or a car or a white picket fence, though all of those things are still very much a part of it in many cases, but instead it's rooted in maximizing your freedom. It's an exciting time, because with more freedom you are free to earn more money, make more deals and build your own dreams.

So if you want to achieve something, anything, you're in the right place. When the Mega Million Jackpot hit more than $500 million recently, job-holders and job-seekers alike dared to dream. What would it be like to become a multi-multi-millionaire overnight, never having to worry about climbing that corporate ladder or looking for that next job?

Except for three lucky winners, all of us came crashing to earth the following morning. We could still chase our dreams, yet those dreams needed to be based in reality.

That's what this book is all about: helping you, the New American Dreamer, reach your goals. If you are lucky enough to be working today (no small feat with so much of the population out of work) you may feel stalled. How do you rev up your career again? Your strategy may be simple, finding a new mentor, for example, or more complicated, actually switching careers.

If you are between jobs, then what do you need to do to stand out from the crowd? You may feel you have done everything possible, but there may be things you have overlooked. Together we will find out what those additional tactics might be and how you can employ them to your advantage.

Technology plays a huge role in the workplace today, whether you want to work for an Internet company or use the Internet to advance your career and business. Everyone—let me repeat that, everyone—needs a presence on the web. You want to manage that image, not a friend or someone who happens to snap your photo at a party. New instruments are now available to help you, but learning how to use sites like Facebook, LinkedIn, Pinterest, Twitter, and others takes some time and effort. Don't worry. You don't have to be 13. We will show you how.

You are here now, that much we know. What better time to get started on your new life, one that doesn't depend on winning the lottery but in working hard to reach your goals. And isn't that strategy really at the heart of reaching the American Dream?

Sit quietly with no electronic device interruptions and imagine a day off of work one year from now. See how each hour passes and what activities you engage in. Don't write anything down and don't judge. Just see the details and see yourself enjoying it. Do this for three minutes, eyes closed or open, every day starting today.

BEFORE YOU CAN START—STOP!

Are you discouraged with the progress of your career? Perhaps what you are doing now is not the career path you had hoped you would follow. You're not alone in your unhappiness. Some polls report that nearly three-quarters of workers are dissatisfied with their jobs. In these trying times, that percentage may be slightly higher. Studies show that people frustrated with their careers usually perform less well than those who are more satisfied, leading to even more discontent in the workplace.

If you love what you do, and make enough money doing it, you probably don't want to change much. But if you are like many people in today's new workplace and you're feeling stuck you may need to get unstuck to advance yourself.

Begin the road to a fulfilling career by going against your instinct to get going. Yes, it's tempting to launch a full blown job search, going on job sites and sending out dozens of resumes. Before you can START—STOP!

Take some time to evaluate your current situation. Suppose you are searching for work. You definitely aren't in the place you want to be so you are probably always looking to get work. It's exhausting, upsetting and pretty lousy all around. First things first – cut yourself some slack. The world tends to talk down to people looking for work as if the reason for it is all about you. Well, it isn't. So many factors can come up and anyone can find themselves on the bottom looking up. So if you're feeling beat up, STOP!

Even if you find yourself jobless beyond your control, you have to believe you can change your situation with hard work and of course with some luck. Because luck seems to find you more easily when you work hard, try focusing on that aspect the most. If you find that watching the news and hearing about how hard it is out there to find a great job brings you down, then do yourself a favor and STOP!

Maybe you have a job but you still feel stifled. What about your job makes you unhappy? While you dislike your overall job, there may be pieces of it that you enjoy. Have you developed bad habits? If so, you may need to STOP and change some habits before you move on.

Look at your daily routine and make one change every week. Walk or take the bus to work one day a week. Skip lunch and take a yoga class one day a week. And if you're one of those Alpha types who is already doing yoga and walking to work and having lunch with colleagues, then maybe you might also benefit from a brief pause. Sometimes even a good habit needs a break from your life before it becomes too robotic. You need stimulation to be enthused and if you're the over-stimulated type you should STOP and change it up for a few weeks.

When you do stop, use that time to look deeper at your goals. What does your ideal job look like? Take 20 minutes each day to visualize where you would like to be. In other words, daydream! Yes, that's right, I said daydream. Believe it or not, daydreaming is the first step on the path to a better job. If you don't believe me, go see the offices at Google or 3M where people are encouraged to daydream and actually get paid to do it!

Stopping allows you to step back and view both the forest and the trees. You may see yourself as part of your company or part of a team. Even if your company's stock is soaring and your team is winning awards, you may still be unhappy. Why? You may have lost sight of your own hopes and dreams, putting them aside in favor of serving a larger cause. "You Inc." should be your focus. No matter where you work, in a large or small company, you are in business for yourself. Sound self-serving? Not at all. If you are happy in what you are doing, everyone benefits—you, your boss, your company, and your clients.

What will it take to make you happy and fulfilled in your job? A better boss? More travel? Taking on more responsibility? If these opportunities are not coming your way, ask yourself why. It may be as simple as asking for a transfer or new responsibilities. Or, it may mean you need to move on.

Feeling a bit more clear-headed by now? Great. This is usually when old fears start knocking on the door. Whatever you do don't answer it. The "I can't's" and "Buts" will be addressed on a case by case basis, so don't go looking for reasons to back down now. There's absolutely nothing to be afraid of, and there are plenty of reasons to believe in yourself. Now you can start to think about what kind of work you should be doing and how to get on with doing it.

If you are ready to change your life, STOPPING can be the key to STARTING.

FINDING YOUR COMPASS

Now that you have dared to dream and STOPPED before starting, it's time to find your compass, in other words, a new direction. Figuring out which way is up can definitely be helpful in your decision-making process. Wondering if that management job at Pfizer you were offered is a lateral move or a leap forward is a common dilemma and the answer depends on many factors.

First know that you have a compass. All this really means is that you need to be honest in three specific areas in your life: where you are, where you are going, and what makes you happy.

If you can be honest about where you are do so but it helps to try it with a friend, because in my experience more often than not people tend to rationalize their displeasures and have a hard time being objective seeing it. Other times people bring with them a tidal wave of complaints that make it hard to see what small good may be achieved and utilized in the future. A trusted friend can help to stop you in your tracks when needed.

I know many people can't tell me much about where they are going and that's normal. Many say they want to get to a position or company but feel like they "can't". So at the risk of sounding annoying, let us all start to chip away at the notion of "can't", especially when it comes to careers. A potential employer can smell "can't" on your breath like vodka and if that is still a part of your vocabulary by the time we get to the interview, you're in trouble. So keep an eye out for "can'ts". Look at your career in terms of what your entire company might be doing in five years or where the companies you like are headed.

Lastly, think about what makes you happy. And keep it simple, this isn't written in stone. I know many people who tell me they can't "decide" on what to do or what makes them happiest - it's not about finding your ideal right now just toss out some things you enjoy doing.

Now look at all those answers. That's your compass. If every day you write down the answer to those three questions you will start to see yourself in new ways. Which is perfect for making a new dream, right?

Take a few minutes to answer the following questions, a mini career choice quiz. The answers may help you determine what you are looking for in your dream job. It will definitely help fill in your compass even more so.

YOU PREFER WORKING:
- A) Standard business hours with weekends off
- B) A more flexible schedule working some weekends or nights

YOU PREFER WORKING:
- A) In a large prestigious company with plenty of room to advance
- B) Smaller companies with more hands on opportunities

YOU PREFER WORKING:
- A) In large teams or as part of teams that do national or prominent work
- B) In smaller teams or alone

YOU PREFER WORKING:
- A) For a determined salary with possible increases based on performance
- B) For a bit less money in exchange for more freedom, flexibility or possible payoff at a later date

YOU PREFER WORKING:

    A) Around similar people who understand and enjoy the same things as yourself

    B) Around all sorts of people who may not always be like you

YOU PREFER WORKING:

    A) In a job where you stay close to home

    B) In a job where you travel as much as 20% of the time or more

YOU PREFER WORKING:

    A) In a job where you use the skills you have

    B) In a job where you may have to be re-trained

YOU PREFER WORKING:

    A) In classic business attire or in a professional manner

    B) In shorts and flip-flops if at all possible

YOU PREFER WORKING:

    A) In a highly driven environment where people work until a job is finished

    B) In a place where there is an understanding that family needs come first

YOU PREFER WORKING:

    A) On long term projects that may take a year or more

    B) On shorter-term projects where you see results quickly

YOU PREFER WORKING:

    A) For a company that is highly successful

    B) For a company that is successful and socially conscious

Now don't worry, there is no score to this test. It just gets you thinking about what is important to you. This test shouldn't decide the fate of your career, but it should tell you something about your direction.

Once you have all of these answers there's one more important question you need to ask yourself: Would you like to work for someone else and be able to focus on your job description or would you prefer to work for yourself, wearing more hats but also being in total control of your own career destiny? Sound like an easy question? Think again. These days there are fewer opportunities to stay with the same company and move up in the hierarchy. That cushy life-long job that used to exist is about as common as a half-price sale at Tiffany's. On the other hand nothing can prepare you for owning your own business. Think you work a lot now? So you see, like any journey, setting your compass in advance is a critical first step.

SELF-BRANDING

There are many who say the origins of personal branding come from Napoleon Hill, the famous author of 'The Law of Success', but if you ask me I say it began around the time humans started competing for food or a mate.

What is personal branding and why do so many people dislike the idea of it? It all begins with what people think branding is. Branding is not a logo, or a tagline or an image or how you comb your hair. It's not any one of those things. Branding is what you promise and how people perceive that promise.

This goes for a company, an organization or a person. It's also important to remember that everyone already has a personal brand because you're being perceived whether you're controlling your promise or not.

Your promise is the sum total of your image, your words, your actions, and what people come to expect from you. That is 'The Promise'. You must control your promise. If you can do so you will find success not only in your career, but in relationships as well because what controlling your promise really translates into is being who you are as honestly as possible.

How others interpret this is another story. Determining how others perceive you often takes a brutal honesty that only an outside voice can feel free enough to say. Often times I am hired to do nothing more than tell the truth about what I see. Insert 'looking in the mirror' analogy here please because it really is the place to start.

So you see personal branding is not about creating an image that is only partly you and makes everyone think you're wonderful. It's about acknowledging your effect on others and then controlling it as best you can.

Obviously you see how branding might be a great tool to have mastered when searching for work. Hiring is done on first impressions because that is all that is available, so if your personal brand is fuzzy or gives off signals counter to what you really represent, then you can't be effective.

Let's break it down into some simple ideas. If you're always dressed flawlessly, your penmanship is perfect and you speak in an articulate and professional manner - but you're always five minutes late for everything - then you should realize people will see someone who is not quite reliable, because many view punctuality as a sign of integrity. In other words be who you are but be consistent. Looking at yourself this closely may even cause you to change things you don't like about yourself.

When it comes to defining you and what we are calling 'your personal brand' there are a few ways to go about it. Break out that pen and paper. Writing forces you to think a bit harder about what you're saying so jot down some ideas to the following questions:

What are your goals?

Are they clearly defined in your mind?

Is it all about a certain job you want to be promoted to, or is it about a salary level you want to achieve?

What drives you?

What are some attributes of those people you aspire to be like?

What makes you unique?

Are there certain professional protocols that need to be acknowledged?

Do you need to understand certain social expectations?

STREET RULE: Always be you, but always know your audience. You can be the least educated person in a group, but if you understand how others value education you can use it to show how much you have accomplished without it, instead of trying to overstate what you do have.

What is your current brand?

What does your behavior, appearance, manner, words and actions all say about you to others?

How do others perceive you?

Can you be honest about what you are promising to each person you meet?

Can you deliver on that promise?

By now if you have answered these questions in writing you should have a good idea of how you need to plan your next moves.

If you need to work on your appearance, or your bad habits, or your body language, or something else, take full responsibility for that challenge and work on yourself. If you want to be someone then start today, not when you get 'there'. There is no 'there'. There is here, so start acting like the person you want to be NOW.

Here are some helpful ways in which to set your personal brand into the sights of others:

> » **DEVISE A PERSONAL MISSION STATEMENT.**
> Will you ever tell it to anyone? I hope not. What I mean

is it exists for you; it should be something that gives your career meaning. What you will get from it that you will show others is an intro or elevator speech. This is the pitch you give to anyone who asks what you're about or what you want to do. It can come in handy in interviews, meetings, at parties or in an actual elevator. It never should sound robotic but it should come from the heart and be a quick way of saying who you are. And it can be one sentence.

» **UTILIZE THE ONLINE WORLD.** Never before can someone do so much with so little as in these times of the New Workplace. Build up your LinkedIn profile, make sure you have a consistent message on your social media platforms; all of it adds up to a huge part of what people think of you nowadays.

» **WRITE LETTERS.** In today's high tech world nothing stands out like a letter in the mail. It also says a lot about who you are. Caring, thoughtful, and someone who understands the importance of the human touch can all go a long way in getting your brand to meet other's approval while also sticking to your values.

» **DRESS WELL.** It doesn't mean spend money, it means taking care of your appearance and being consistent. If you're a hippie and in an industry where it's acceptable then wear shorts to work, but be consistent and wear distinctive shorts. If you are fastidious and always need a pocket square then have a different one every day; make it a small signature not just something you do.

So you see building a personal brand teaches you that it really isn't about marketing yourself at all. It's about BEING you. If you can do that successfully you will surely find success!

LAUNCHING WHILE YOU WORK

One more step in your journey and it's often the hardest. What to do if you have a job and yet aren't sure if you should take the plunge and go after something else? And if you decide to, then how does one do it? It might seem daunting but if you are not feeling fulfilled in your job then it is time to reflect on your current path.

How to tell if it's time to look for another job can be as easy as being honest about your level of happiness, but it can also mean looking at other factors. Is the company you work for going through major changes? Is the industry you work in sending jobs out of the country a little at a time? You want to look at your situation from every angle before making a decision.

Let's say you do a mental inventory and you find you aren't totally sure but would be interested in another job if it was better in some way. Or better yet, let's say you should never stop looking for a better opportunity. Then remind yourself that all you have done is agree to window shop and now you can set about developing a plan.

An employer can fire you for even saying you hate your job so start by keeping this secret away from everyone at work. I mean *everyone* because people talk. It's natural to want to vent but you need to do that at home to your spouse or best friend. But even if you don't hate your job, it's important to keep things to yourself because if you are fired then your job search takes on a desperate quality that leaves you at a disadvantage.

You want to be searching for a job while you have a job for many reasons, the primary one being that you need to pay the bills while you look. This will alleviate much of the stress that occurs during a job search when you have to worry about money and security. Another reason is that being unemployed can make someone less confident, which translates to all sorts of problems in interviews and in salary negotiations. So do not resign or quit in haste.

Here are some things to remember if you're looking for work while you work.

> » **Never look for work on the company's computer.** You would think I wouldn't have to say this, but I do. For those who don't know, computers log every click and the employer has more than every right to look at what you're up to if you do it on their computer. So don't.

> » **If you must send out emails and resumes** during work hours do so on your lunch time and go to a wireless location outside of the office.

> » **Don't use your current job email addresses to apply to other jobs.** And don't call from their phones either. Again should I have to say this?

> » **Don't talk about it to others at work.** Even when you think people should do the right thing, their careers are at stake. If they think you're leaving and the company is paying their bills, which allegiance are they going to take? Exactly.

> » **Don't talk openly about job searches on social media.** Same thing as doing it in the office.

» **USE REFERENCES THAT COME FROM PAST JOBS** not the current position.

» **GO TO INTERVIEWS IN BUNCHES SO YOU AREN'T OUT OF THE OFFICE A TON** leading to suspicion. Don't come in on a half day from 'dropping the kids off at school' dressed in interview clothes. Try to schedule two or three interviews in one day to make it easier on you and your employer.

» **DO YOUR JOB.** By this I mean do not start to slack off because you are leaving. Not only will it make them suspicious but it just won't make you look good down the road.

If you work in a flexible position and can work around it to find other opportunities, that's great. Even if you are locked in to a tight schedule, you can make inroads that you can follow up on your own time.

The best way to find a job is to know someone who has one, so even if you make that extra effort to meet people on behalf of your current job, it may turn out to benefit you in the long run.

Hand out business cards, make lunch dates, stay in contact with people and generally be more social and then keep those ears perked ready for any hint at a lead.

The key to remember through all of this is that you shouldn't be sitting at your desk feeling helpless. Most of the time there are things you can do to further your career and ultimately your life. You just need to be resourceful in the way you do things and most of all keep your integrity. Don't look for a job on company time because it's not the right thing to do plain and simple. However if you can do things, even little things, to start the process and it doesn't affect your duties, then do so but play by the rules and don't let on to anyone.

As we said in the beginning, you might take a good look at what is out there and find that you have a terrific situation and return to your work more appreciative and better for it. Either way you should pursue your own instincts and create your own New American Dream.

WHAT YOUR EMAIL SAYS ABOUT YOU

After taking the quiz in Chapter 3, you may have some new ideas about your future. You feel energized and want to hop on your computer and get started on your journey. Just a minute! No, I'm not stopping you this time. We just need to strategize.

Let's talk about emails.

I think it's safe to say that you have an email address. Most likely you use it to email your friends, your family, and maybe even co-workers. Until now you probably haven't had reason to give it much thought. After today, I hope you will.

Think of your email address as your name. Have a nice ring to it? Even with the .com ending? I say to view this email address as your digital name because that's exactly what it is. Whenever you send or receive emails, people see your name. It's free advertising for YOU. But it's also a quick way of telling a bit about someone - if you're in the new American workplace that is.

Emails come with cache; they can show cleverness, or even creativity. But what do you want an employer to think of when they think of you? Let's look at your current email and see.

How do you put together this email address? Pick your full name or first initial and last name and put them together as in judyjones or jjones. If your name is common, chances are that someone with your name got there first. You may have to add something to your name, the two-letter abbreviation of your state, for example, such as judyjonesny, or a two-digit number, judyjones67. Yes, you can use a dot (judy.jones) but just be aware that the dot will have to be very clear in all communication or you will lose email to that vast digital no man's land. (Don't use a dot.)

It seems like I shouldn't have to say this but I will: for your business email, don't use any nicknames or, even worse, an address that displays a less serious side of your personality, such as pokershark98@yahoo or kimtequila@msn.

If you're determined not to leave your playful side behind, then sign up for a few email addresses. I suggest three—one for business, one for your social side, and one to handle all that junk mail you receive. No, you won't have to check them all every day and you can have all your mail forwarded to one email address easily enough. The idea is to have one email address for business as we discussed today, one for personal use such as kimtequila@msn, and then one for those deals online that make you give up your email address so they can then send you endless amounts of junk.

Next you need to pick a provider such as Google, Yahoo, MSN, or any number of other choices. My advice is to go straight to Google and sign up for a Gmail account. No, I don't have stock in the company. The fact is simple: They have a great email system and a set of supporting tools that are easy to use. It also says something about you that you are with an innovative company as opposed to say, an AOL email which to some comes across as something from the "olden days".

There is one other option and that is to purchase your name at a registry and create a professional looking judy@judyjones.com address. There are many companies that do this but a few popular ones are www.godaddy.com, www.register.com, and www.networksolutions.com..

Once you set up your email you should think about setting up an email signature. This just means it will say whatever you choose at the end of each email. My suggestion here is again to show restraint.

If you currently have a job, then this might be a good signature:

Judy Jones
Wonder Pets Inc.
Accounting Assistant
555-555-5555

If you do not have a job or don't wish to advertise where you currently work simply try:

Judy Jones
555-555-5555

Do not put your home phone in your email. It's just not a great idea, emails get forwarded and it's better to put a cell phone number if possible.

OK, judyjones59@gmail, nice work. With this out of the way, we will continue with our journey.

Email Providers List

> » Gmail

> » Yahoo

> » MSN

> » AOL

> » Zoho

» iCloud

» Mail.com

» Mac

HOW THE DAY BREAKS

f you're looking for your next move and feel the pressures that go along with that effort, you may make decisions solely based on the situation you're in now instead of creating a new set of needs and wants based on your true life goals.

Not everyone has the time to fully realize what they want at the moment a new opportunity arises so the key is to move closer toward your goals while staying open to anything and everything.

First let's talk about your goals and wants.

I find it valuable to ask people to describe things they want in life and then ask why they want them. The answers are usually interesting because they often change during the answer itself as the person realizes that what they are describing isn't exactly what they really want. Having an understanding of how to choose between what you want, what you think you want and what you should want if you had known you could want it is an important first step. OK maybe I ought to explain that.

Whenever I ask people what they want from their careers, many answer in general terms, repeating what they have always said or explaining what they think will make them successful. Answers range from "money" to "power" to "being satisfied with what I do everyday", all fine answers but what's missing are the details.

What does "being satisfied everyday" mean to you? Does it mean working really hard on something that wins awards or saves whales? Does it mean traveling around the world attending meetings or does it mean writing the great American novel? Define it because it will come to define you if you don't.

Of course with so little time to daydream (try anyway!) we often don't think of options that might be out there. Jump start your brain by thinking of all the people you admire and list what they do. Maybe you won't become Secretary of State or First Violinist but perhaps there are ways to be around your ideal job in a supporting capacity that satisfies you. If you find your career passions are more financially influenced, then that alone can help suggest certain industries over others. The point is give it some thought - in different ways than before.

Or try this: Did you ever go to work with one of your parents when you were a child? If so, you may have spent time in the corner drawing pictures and watching the goings on of a world unbeknownst to you until then. Maybe you even got to sit at the big desk and might have even picked up your parent's accounting ledger and screamed "THIS IS ME!" Or maybe like most children you went home with an upset stomach from consuming mountains of free doughnuts in the break room.

Well what if we could create a time machine that would send you back to that same office to see just how that job is really performed? Hey good news! There actually are tools out there that you can use that are even better than that old time machine idea. One I like is called vault.com, a site that serves as an online career media center. The insightful feature they run called 'Day in the Life' is an hour-by-hour report of the average day for almost any profession you can think of under the sun. Have you ever wondered what an assistant wind developer for a power company actually does? Or how many hours an entry-level scientist works? Maybe you were interested in learning about a typical day for a magazine ad sales rep? At vault.com, you can choose from an ever-growing bank of professions and their hourly breakdown. Even if you don't find your ideal job you will see that there are so many opportunities out there that you may not have even considered.

This type of information, placed alongside your lifestyle choices, can be half of the treasure map to career happiness. We tend to think of things like status, industry growth, and that little thing called money when we start to formulate ideas about a direction in our career, yet the happiest people love what they do on an hour-to- hour basis and make enough to enjoy their time off. A 'Day in the Life' exercise can also spotlight certain aspects of a career that you thought you liked. Not a fan of meetings? Then maybe being a marketing director isn't for you. Or maybe you are a bit weary of working within large teams? Then aiming to be a corporate interior designer isn't a good choice. Love the rush of 'the chase'? Perhaps the stock market is the place for you.

The vault.com site is more than just this one feature. Snoop around a bit. You can read advice on everything from career changes to typical interview questions for a specific job. It's a great resource for those still wondering what they want at this stage of the journey.

Of course there are other great career oriented websites out there and we will get to a directory of some sites later. Start with sites like smartbrief.com where you can sign up for industry related newsletters and over a few weeks learn a ton about numerous industries.

Once you have even a smidge of an idea of what you might consider there's always the road you are on now to mull over as well. Make a list of things you like about your current situation and use that as another way of seeing what's important to you when the dust clears. Do you like the daily routine? Where is it taking you? Do you feel your potential is being expressed as best as can be? Just remember, no job is perfect and no job is focused on your happiness all day long every day, but a job is much like a relationship in that if over time, you aren't getting your needs met, then sooner or later it will most likely be time for a change.

Make sure you investigate your possible choices now, rather than a month into your new position. And when you consider your future, be as specific as possible about what you want in your mind, even though it will never be that perfect in real life. Just define it for yourself. The more you know, the better your chances for success, however you define it.

E-LEARNING FOR E-XCELLENCE

The one thing that many people see as a barrier to career advancement is additional training and education. Oftentimes we see ourselves as the king or queen of our domain but deep down we know that if we were to leave our current position, it would take some new training or it might even be necessary to further our education to remain at the same level or to go further ahead. This is part of the New World Workplace, where the one most important idea is to do what I call ABP - always - be - pushing.

Even if your current situation is sugary sweet, maybe you're married to the owner so you definitely have job security, but what about your ability to compete with others outside of the company in terms of hiring the best people or finding the best vendors? As we said before: your productivity matters. So even if you aren't searching for a job you can benefit from doing some learning, right?

But if you feel like there is no way you could ever get that necessary training because of the cost or lack of time, then you are especially made for this New World Workplace! So perk up because in the age of the New World Workplace technology plays a key role, so much so that now you don't even have to go to class to further your career.

E-Learning has been around almost since the dawn of the Internet but the current state of offerings presents a far more complex and valuable set of opportunities - if only for the right person.

Let's start with defining e-Learning and it's more utilized progeny, online education. E-Learning simply means using electronic technology to enhance the learning experience. Ever use an electronic whiteboard? That's e-Learning. But in the instance of helping you further your career there are some ways e-Learning has taken the lead in providing degrees and training that can help anyone with computer access grow within their career. We will discuss those below.

Let's address the first thing many wonder about online degrees and that is, are they worth anything? Do employers take them seriously, do they give you the education they promise and are they for you?

In 2011 the Sloan Consortium did a study showing that though many institutions remained on the sidelines as far as online degrees were concerned, there were over six million people taking at least one online course. With those kinds of numbers growing exponentially, it is only a matter of time before this type of learning becomes, dare we say, `normal'. Couple this growth with that same study's findings that 77% of academic leaders say that e-Learning outcomes are equal to or better than face-to-face classrooms.

Whether or not any individual company or person weighs an online degree against a brick and mortar or traditional degree and sees it as insufficient is up to that individual, however what we are seeing is an ever-increasing acceptance that should one day lead to an across the board acknowledgment of the degree's value. Will every HR manager approve of your online degree? Perhaps not by itself, but here is what you need to remember: if that is your one degree and you have no experience and nothing else that says `hire me' then you probably won't get the job. However, if you have experience, perhaps another degree or some other schooling, skills that are pertinent and a great personality, will that degree stop you or help you? The answer is that it will most likely help you a lot - especially compared to that same candidate without any degree.

You cannot believe how little people care where you went to school once you get a job and become good at it. But please don't tell that to anyone else because if that ever gets out nobody save for the few with large amounts of disposable income would venture to a private university. As state colleges and other educational methods become more appealing, the online degrees should start to become more respected.

Online degrees are however just one avenue for gaining a technological education. Here is an overview of the types of ways in which to better yourself:

MOOCS OR MASSIVELY-OPEN ONLINE COURSES

These are classes that are offered to anyone with access, and in some cases these are offerings from the world's best schools such as Princeton, Stanford, even MIT. The one catch is that these courses are not available for college credit, but instead are solely for the access to learning.

DOOCS OR DISTRIBUTED-OPEN COLLABORATIVE COURSES

These are relatively newer and actually challenge the traditional roles of the instructor and are generally against having one centralized syllabus but rather distribute expertise through a collaborative effort. Again, no accredited degree.

PRIVATE ONLINE PROGRAMS

These are fantastically innovative and changing the face of education but do not have the clout to offer degrees. Khan Academy, Udacity, Lynda, W3Schools and others offer courses that have no suggested syllabus but offer creative and inspiring courses via online lectures. These I recommend even if you aren't pursuing a degree. And many of these are FREE or inexpensive.

ONLINE COLLEGES

These online colleges that offer lectures and teaching interactive via the Internet are the places where you can get a degree. The University of Phoenix, Aspen University, and now Kaplan University are offering degrees, have teachers who hold 'virtual office hours' and even have financial aid. Well known nationally accredited Colleges and Universities are just now in the process of developing courses for credit, but at this time it is more the exception rather than the rule.

A word to the wise here: I am not endorsing any of these methods or schools. You can do the homework but overall each of these is worth a look if you feel you need to go back to school and do not have time or are not located close to a campus.

The thing to remember is that there are so many opportunities out there these days that nobody should ever stop learning. Try a course on Khan Academy to see if online learning is even something you might be interested in. Speak with your company before signing up for anything and if you are using it to make a career leap talk to others in the field to make sure these steps are for you. In general however, it is always going to be helpful if you are pursuing your learning as hard as you pursue your career goals.

9

LET'S RESUME OUR DISCUSSION

The resume as we know it is going the way of the typewriter. It's in an evolutionary phase as we speak, transforming itself from a documented list of work and education experience into a dynamic tool for presenting oneself. Someday a resume might take the form of a 3D autobiography. But it's not quite there yet.

It still needs to have certain components so that everyone from an HR director to a career web portal can process it. It also still needs to be accurate and presented without a single mistake. But before we get to that let's take a step back.

If I asked for everyone reading this article to email their resume to me, I imagine I would be fairly impressed with many of them all for different reasons. Some may show great accomplishments while others will show time spent with Fortune 500 companies or prominent educations. So you're thinking, with so many wonderful resumes out there what's the problem? Well therein lies the problem! With so many good ones out there, how does yours stand out from the pack and get you that interview?

Good question.

Now for those of you who are running your own business or considering it, you probably think you're off the hook when it comes to resumes. The truth is that in some instances business owners do go without using resumes, but I would bet that most everyone has one, even if it's on their backup hard drive in the garage. Why? The simple act of writing the resume makes you think, truly think, about "YOU Inc." and what you bring to any business situation and it can become the outline for a great company bio.

Resumes can have many components but let's start with the core four:

1) Contact Information – Your name, partial address, phone numbers and email address belong at the top. Now I say "partial address" for this reason: especially when sending resumes to an unknown address, consider that resumes float around carelessly and any prospective employer doesn't necessarily need your home address. It should be enough at that stage to give your town, state and zip code while leaving the street address until you get to fill in an application. Also make sure all your spelling is accurate and of course use a professional email address preferably justyourname@somethingotherthanhotmail. I have nothing against hotmail but it limits attachment sizes, can 'spam' your OUTGOING emails and what is worse, 'hotmail' just doesn't make you sound like a serious professional.

2) A Summary or Objective – I have to include this at this point in time though I believe these openings are headed for extinction. If you feel you can do without an Objective or a Summary then do so - every industry has different resume expectations and this is just an overview. But depending on the industry, this section is your first chance to actually SPEAK, so choose every word carefully. Write this and then re-write it and then re-write it again. Show it to someone you trust without your resume attached and see how it reads. It should get a point across without sounding arrogant.

3) Work Experience – So much info, so little time! Again every word counts. Here is where you need to describe everything you did with active verbs and be specific whenever possible. Active verbs are words that show progressive action, describing the aspects of your role that resulted in some positive result for the company or organization. Quantify these verbs whenever possible. Keywords are now also a major part of making a resume and not just because the digital world wants them. Think of keywords as their name implies - they are words that employers 'key' on and they are also industry relevant. For

instance in the case of an architect's resume certain certifications are going to be mandatory and employers will key on those first before even looking at other items. These same words also result in digital `keywords' that allow career sites and employment web portals to sort resumes before a human even sees them! So include important words that are going to be meaningful to the employer you wish to work for. And of course in this section make sure you have an accurate list of all experiences, dates, and supervisors.

4) Education & Training – Always necessary, and yet another chance to shine. Show your school, but remember, giving dates of attendance allows them to guess your age. Make quick reference to your major or course of study, your degree achieved and anything unusual that might attract those eyeballs. And if you are less than proud of your academic life? No problem. List what you did do and then have something to say about your education that is positive in an interview. This comes later. So yes, you can make up for it in other ways – just don't lie - ever!

There are obviously more parts to a great resume, with many industries demanding different requisites. At the least, you need to know what you are applying for so that your resume is inclined to be well received. And if you are going into a new industry then doing a little research can help you find out everything you need to know. First off, try perusing www.indeed.com under the 'Find Resumes' section. It's a great site and we will use it again later in your search. Another place to see some sample resumes is a site by Susan Ireland at www.susanireland.com. I don't know Susan but she appears to be a one-woman resume machine and she has some good resources on her site.

I know some of you will make a great resume that reflects your experiences and others may find it harder to do so and still be happy with what they have to present, so the temptation is always there to fudge a little on things you did or didn't do. We all show ourselves in the best light possible (I hope!) on our resume and there is nothing wrong with that - but there are times when someone might be willing to falsify a resume on purpose to get ahead. I don't want to sound like it's coming from a moral point of view because this is, after all, your business. When my clients ask if they should fudge that not-so-real-promotion at their old firm to bump up their credentials I tell them that it just isn't worth it. If your company grossed $499M under your supervision and you want to round it up to $500M that's not going to send off any alarms, but if you willingly deceive people, you may eventually get caught, and if you were in the running for a job, you won't be in the running for long. With resumes being sent around in emails people do check on what you say. So my advice is - always stick to the truth.

On the other hand you should choose your words carefully and strategically so that you communicate yourself in the best way possible and make even your ordinary experiences sound like amazing adventures! If you do that, even without a ton of experience or an Ivy League diploma, you too can get ahead.

10

GO FOR IT

magine if you will, your resume is finished, looking as if it were written on parchment paper in gold leaf, and I tell you to take it, roll it up, put it into an old wine bottle and toss it into the sea. Maybe some of you would expect that from me by now, but what I really want to convey is that resumes alone are about as likely to be found by that one special person as the wine bottle bobbing around the surf - unless you have a plan.

The resume we use nowadays was created in 1482 (yes you read that right) by none other than Leonardo Da Vinci when he applied for a court position at the House of Sforza. Da Vinci's brilliance in all things is yet again applied here as his newly invented cover letter/resume hybrid goes on to succinctly describe himself in such a way as to show his maximum value to Ludovico Sforza at that time the ruler of Milan, besieged by French armies. Everything Da Vinci says in the resume is about what he can do for Ludovico in times of war - while only mentioning his brilliant artistic skills near the bottom of the list because he knew that wasn't what Lodovico was looking for at that time. Talk about a gutsy self-marketing genius.

The resume was and always will be a self-promotional marketing tool. It can do anything from introducing you to securing an interview to getting you a position. In its contemporary format it should have the ability to do all three of those things. The question of how is a bit more tricky and one should look to basic marketing principles for help.

Here is a basic marketing tip that applies to almost every situation I can think of:

Have a plan!

In poor marketing, actions are put into place without any thought about goals and strategy. In average marketing, generic actions are put into place as one-size-fits all solutions. In good marketing, no actions take place before you have a goal and a strategy.

Final analysis: Have a plan and strategies.

This can be done quite easily just by asking yourself: what jobs you want (your goal) and how best to get them (your strategy). As we discussed in the last chapter there are some building blocks to any good contemporary resume depending on your industry. What comes next are your strategies for getting this resume to the right people. When you look at how you will get this resume to people who can help you, one method that stands out today is the Internet submission. Chances are many of you will have to send a resume online either through email or at a company website or job board.

When using your resume online there are some new considerations to be aware of that can affect your strategy. The term Search Engine Optimization or "SEO" involves the use of giving words a value depending on their pertinence to a particular search. If you are searching for a car mechanic for instance, words like `car', `mechanic', and phrases like `automobile shop' are all words heavily associated with that search. Other words such as `new tires' or `oil change' are valuable but maybe less so since those are specific to those needs only. On the other hand, if you specifically need new tires or an oil change those words then become more valuable as more people will search for them. These words are all called `keywords' because they are `key' in finding what you want.

Why is this important to you? Because employers are now using search-style software that only allows those resumes with certain `keys' to be moved forward meaning if you don't have them, you might not get your resume seen by a human. To have your resume become known to the search engine tools that employers use and more importantly to make sure that when it is found it hits all the right 'keys' in the mind of the reader and gets you an interview, you will need to insert these words as they apply to your experiences, allowing your resume to be seen as 'sufficiently qualified' to be moved forward.

To find those keywords go to that job site called www.indeed.com once again and take a look at your competition. Hit 'search resumes' and see words that are used over and over in other good resumes and look closely how they are used.

Many keywords come in one of a few categories:

>> Job titles

>> Names of industry-specific tools or knowledge

>> Special industry descriptors or value items

>> Names of software or hardware that one needs training to utilize

>> Special certifications that are a pre-requisite

To show you an easy example here, if I were to make a bartending resume some keywords I might use would be: 'wine knowledge', 'customer service', and 'T.I.P.S. Certification' because these are all elements in the best resumes I have seen. You can also find out what are keywords for your resume by asking someone in that industry.

The next thing to pay close attention to is ensuring the conversion of descriptions of your past experience into stronger verb terms and then, if possible, quantifying it. It is always better to hear you were the lead on a project and not just 'part of' it, or that you were the reason for an increase in sales by 12% and not just 'assisting'. Once again, never imply or say anything untrue. But make sure you say what you did and if it can be measured, say so. Make the verb important, at least as important as you were to the process. One thing I notice is that people tend to under-sell themselves and often have no idea that they are doing so. If you were part of a team that helped increase sales, then say it and by how much - don't be shy. If you can put a number on it, then do so, just make sure that you can also easily discuss it in detail in an interview and that you haven't misled anyone.

Another important part of your strategy to get noticed is to know what is going on at the very moment you send that resume out. So do some research! Let's suppose you want to become a financial analyst. You have a resume ready and maybe it's tremendously impressive, but even within industries, hiring trends tend to change with the wind and what was in demand last year might already be SO last year. Regulations in that industry may have changed and even if they haven't, perhaps wording styles have. So do your research and be current.

OK, great. Take a deep breath; this stuff is hard I know. Give yourself some credit. If you want to have a little fun with it, then visit www.rezscore.com, a site that uses metrics measuring such things as keywords and gives you an assessment of the quality of your resume. Just promise me you won't take it too seriously.

SEARCHING FOR YOURSELF

Two of the most important facts to know about yourself are your credit score and your online presence. You can be hindered by errors or bad items on both, but the good news is you can also change or correct errors or problems on both - but only if you look.

When it comes to job searches remember one thing - your potential employer is actively looking into your world and that means your online presence.

We know how nosey everyone is these days, constantly looking up each other online, checking on old friends and past co-workers to see what they might be up to. It's all quite harmless and in some cases can rekindle an old friendship. The thing is those same photos of you in your New Year's Eve hat if taken out of context might be seen by a potential employer who might form an opinion of you based on them. So take a closer look at what could be a valuable asset - your web presence should be a self-marketing tool in addition to a social tool - and make sure it's not a liability.

First search for yourself on Google, Bing and Facebook and see what comes up. No need to go more than three pages deep on any search unless there is a ton of information on you out there. When doing so make sure you are not logged in to the sites as that will distort your searches. Then you will see exactly what others see when they look you up. Also search for yourself in the images sections of each search tool as well. LinkedIn and Twitter accounts might come up in the search results, but if not, search for yourself on those as well and see what your account looks like to others.

Let's say you do a search for yourself and you see something you don't quite like. This happens more than you think and there are ways to deal with it. First of all, remain calm. Before you leap to all sorts of conclusions consider the motivations of the people responsible for posting the information, decide whether they did it thinking you wouldn't mind, or if these postings are malicious. If it's a newspaper article about your very public divorce, then that is up there to stay - though there are ways to handle that situation to minimize the damage. Many times this has something to do with Facebook. If you see something you do not like on Facebook, first try and contact the person by email and nicely state why you believe the information is not for public consumption or untrue and ask if the person would be willing to take it down.

If they are uncooperative you can also file a complaint with Facebook, but there is no guarantee the site will do anything. If it is really a serious offense, there is a number for Facebook headquarters (650) 543-4800 but officials will tell you they do not offer this type of help over the phone. The best bet is to press the prompt for 'other inquiries' in the automated menu and leave a message. For those of you out there deleting your Facebook accounts as you read this, don't worry - these types of instances are rare. Most times simply asking a friend or someone you know to take down that photo of you in Mickey Mouse ears will be enough.

If you see something you do not like about yourself on a private site, you will have to contact the webmaster or site owner. The webmaster's email is sometimes on the site itself; always check the bottom of the screen. Not sure who is running the site or whom to contact? Try this website to see if they are listed: www.whois.domaintools.com. If it's listed look for 'Admin Email' and contact them at that address. If they aren't listed, there will be a technical contact with an email address available. If you saw it on Google you can also go to Google Content Removal with your plea, but it's very time consuming, so be patient.

Like I said most of the time simply asking someone to change something is enough, but for those rare instances when it isn't, you can take further action. I suggest contacting a lawyer who can interpret and report Terms and Conditions Violations for you.

You may be feeling fortunate when you search for yourself online and find nothing, nada, zero. Not so fast. Under the universal rules of balance being an optimal state, you actually do want something to come up when you search for yourself. You may not want derogatory information about you on the Internet, but you do need to have a presence online or people will think one of the following about you: you're not a social person; you are too out of touch with modern digital life to even have some presence; or you have never done anything. Not a pretty picture.

How do you create and manage your own online presence? It takes an effort but it can be done fairly easily. First of all Facebook can show a lot about you but I usually recommend keeping that page locked except for viewing by friends and connections. It's not you but the accidental posting from an over-enthusiastic friend that can usurp your effort, so why leave it open? Other sites are far better for you to be seen on and though it depends on your tastes and your professional image here are a few:

> » Be an expert - go to sites that pertain to an area where you want to be seen as an expert and make intelligent comments on boards and in forums. Answering a Yahoo question is a quick way to show your thinking and be seen as tech-savvy. And it's easy.

> » Start a blog - this takes time but will be a great display of your abilities and add a lot to your image online. It doesn't have to consist of daily entries to be relevant. A good blog can be three sentences twice a week - just make it smart and related to your chosen field. And by searching the Internet anyone can find free blogging tools and be up and running in just a few minutes. One caution

- don't start a blog unless you have ten entries pre-written. It's far better not to blog at all rather than show that you start things and then do not follow-through. Pre-written entries give you a head start.

» Linkedin.com - which we will use as our online presence template and build a page in the next few chapters.

So if you need to take steps to remove offending information and photographs that could damage your reputation, act now to do so. The next step is going to build some impressive content about yourself online, controlling in a very positive manner what people see and think about you.

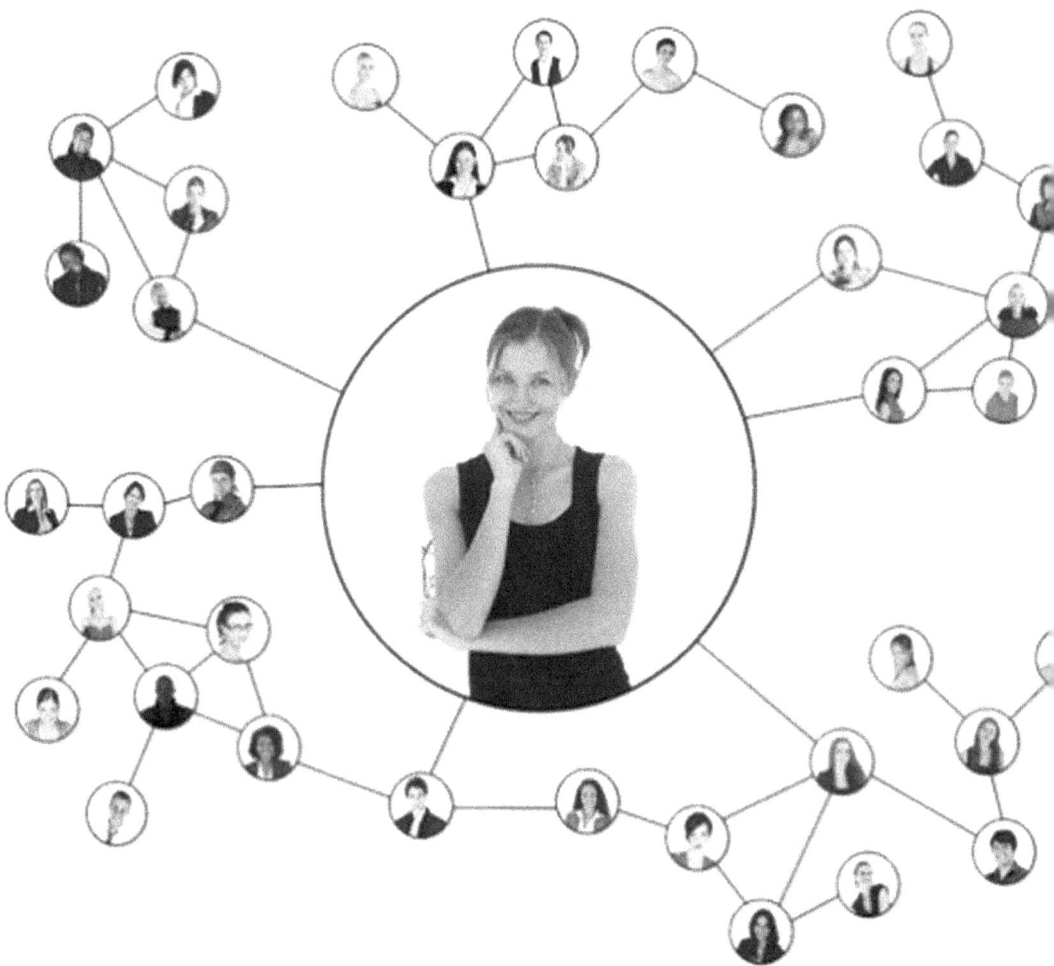

LINKING UP

I know what you're thinking, you searched high and low and you found next to nothing about yourself online and now you're afraid that I want you to spend months building an online identity just to get a job, and this is all too much to overcome. Not to worry. You couldn't be more wrong.

Here's what we do need to do: paint a picture of yourself that you would want people to see, doing it efficiently and quickly. Never picked up a brush before? Don't own an easel? Follow me to get a hold of your inner Rembrandt.

Of all the sites online where your identity might pop up during a search one stands alone as the most professional. (However the Internet being what it is this could change in an instant.) Right now, LinkedIn is the site many employers check first.

There are various philosophies on creating an online presence and as many ways to do it, so remember we are just going to go ahead with LinkedIn for now but feel free to expand beyond it.

Why LinkedIn? No, I don't own stock. Initially LinkedIn touted itself as a social network for business professionals, yet slowly evolved into something more. For many hiring managers, LinkedIn has become an important part of the hiring process.

Remember that third email address you set up just for a place to receive various email offers and complete necessary sign-ins for jobs in our story about setting up your emails? Well now is the time to pull that one out and sign up for LinkedIn just to look around. The sign up process is easy; just enter your name, email address and password.

Once you are registered you should take your time and look around. Don't create a profile yet - look at people whom you think you would be competing against in the workplace and study their profiles. How do they list their work experience? What do they emphasize? What do they list as accreditations and awards? How many connections do they have on average? Do they have many recommendations? What are their photos like? This information is important because every industry is different and nothing I say can work for everyone so do your homework on this.

Also search for positions you might want some day and see how those people present themselves.

Once you think you're ready, you can start to create a profile or delete the account by going to LinkedIn's 'close your account' section and then rejoin with your primary email address.

Before you get too excited with designing your new profile remind yourself that creating a good profile as opposed to creating 'just a profile', takes a little time in some cases. Later we will deal with the choosing of your photo and other items because they need to present you in the best light possible. For now let's stick to the nuts and bolts of it.

NAME AND TITLE: First, get your name up there and capitalize the first letter in each part of your name, not all caps and not all lower case. Next – and this is *tres importante,* is that it asks you to enter your "professional headline" which will be positioned directly under your name and be a huge part of how people see you, and where and how you come up in searches. Think about it from all angles. Use it to communicate value – as an example, a person working as an executive hiring manager but who has interests in running a human resource division, might be better explained here as a 'Human

Resources Manager', or something that translates across industries. Be honest and be sharp. Keep the hyphens to a minimum but if you have various titles here is the place to put the top two.

EMPLOYMENT EXPERIENCE: Lists of past employment can actually be a little longer in scope on LinkedIn than on your one page resume. But don't go all the way back to your newspaper route. What I suggest is copying the information directly from your resume onto the site. If you think it shows more of you to list experiences further back then do so, but do not elaborate on anything over 15 years in the past. And a good way to present your experience is to think of this as your resume - for the quick reading online viewer - so keep it fairly simple. Listing the job title, two or three lines about your accomplishments at the position, and the amount of years worked are fine, all in order of last job first just as on your resume. When you finish it should look like your resume with those few extra jobs listed from way back when and with a tighter description under each job. One thing to remember - if you change your resume you need to change your LinkedIn profile.

ACCREDITATIONS AND ACCOLADES: Fill in the education section because not only is it important, but others who went to your school will search for you. Alumni ties are a great way to find and get work. Depending on your type of work you might need to list certifications or titles. If you are an architect, you want to express memberships in The American Institute of Architects (AIA) or people will not even consider you for work. Also hit the specialties section, but be cautious. Don't list 'juggling knives' unless you are looking for related work AND want that to be part of an interview – because it will be if you list it. If you have a great skill that is fun to talk about, list it but remember - more is not always better. One thing you should consider is that you DO list all languages, software knowledge and union certifications.

Now I know the attraction of these sites is the connecting part and you will be doing that in short time. But before you make a friend or go 'linking in' there's something to consider: are you joining this site to connect with people you already know and strengthen those relationships, or are you trying to meet new people and make new networking contacts?

People have become ardent supporters of either philosophy because some people take offense to connecting with a stranger. They feel it cheapens the site's value and is perhaps in some way deceptive. The battle lines have been drawn for these two camps and people choose whole social networks based on these two philosophies, which some of us (who, me?) find fairly entertaining. As you see some have even chosen to become 'LIONS' (LinkedIn Open Networker) while others vehemently oppose but have yet to come up with a clever acronym for 'TIGERS'. I will only say this - you should come up with your own reasons for joining, but not feel compelled to be so black and white on the issue. Why can't it be a bit of both? After all aren't you joining these sites to meet people? I respect both sides of the issue so do what feels right and also know that you can always change your mind.

TIME FOR YOUR CLOSE-UP

S taying with the LinkedIn leg of our journey let's get to a fun yet critical part of creating your profile, whether on LinkedIn or any other site: the photo. Images have long dominated the eye's attention and online it's no different. The photo not only is the first draw, it's also the last, giving the eye clues as to who you are and how believable you will be to others. If a picture says a thousand words this one needs to start with the phrase, 'hire me'.

This photo is a key piece to your profile. To see how it fits, let's step back for a moment and see an even bigger picture and take a quick peek at personal branding.

Let's say you went to the store and saw a logo on their signage and thought, 'that is a really cool image, I will remember that.' Or better yet, 'I can relate to what that image is saying.' Many people feel that way when they see the iconic Apple logo designed by Rob Janoff or when they see an image of Michael Jordan dunking a ball wearing a pair of sneakers. Now let's say you went to another state and saw an Apple store with a totally different sign or logo or sneakers with Michael Jordan in street clothes on the heel of some shoe. No good.

Personal branding is something we do whether we try or not, it's something I have begun to work into our journey here and it's important enough to know about but not be obsessed with. It simply means showing a consistent face representing a promise you can keep. You want to be known as reliable? BE reliable but also show reliable qualities. All of this will help you not only in finding a job - but also in climbing the ladder.

When it comes to branding, consistency is essential. Therefore choosing an image that best represents you and that is going to be consistently out there representing you is hard but satisfying. It allows you not to panic when someone needs a photo for a corporate bio or a presentation. You will have already picked the photo you use everywhere. So make this choice and stick to it. Though you can change it later and in time should, it's more about being consistent across a span of months.

When looking to make your way in the business world you can help yourself by finding an image that shows you as professional, presentable and as someone who knows how to choose a professional photo. Once the photo has met those criteria - and only after that point - you can get `creative' with your online photo.

Your best bet is to simply take a great color photo of your face, looking happy, and just start there. Smiling is always a plus. Dress exactly as you would for a job interview or an important meeting, whatever that means for your industry. Keep to a bust shot, nobody needs to see your shoes in a small profile picture. Business attire, smile, shot from bust level up - these types of photos almost always work best for a LinkedIn profile unless your last job was at Barnum & Bailey Circus, in which case red nose and wig are fine.

Of course there are exceptions and degrees of separation that are tactical and worthwhile. If you're in a creative position such as graphic design, you might do something tasteful but keep it simple. Sometimes simply going 'all B&W' is enough to stand out in a distinct and interesting way. But if you're searching for a position on Wall Street or looking for a partner for your dental practice, my advice is to first keep it simple.

Here are some things to avoid:

SHOTS OF YOU IN AN ACTIVITY. Please no shots of you sitting on a park bench eating lunch. Nothing from a photo booth in a mall. None of you at the opening night of *Lion King* either. Seriously keep the focus on your face, no body shots and no funky backdrops.

LOOKING ANYTHING BUT PROFESSIONAL, INTELLIGENT AND CONFIDENT. That means anything slightly hysterical, shocking, silly or clever should be best kept to your photo album. Here it's better to just smile or appear neutral if smiling is difficult for you. (In which case we need to talk.)

SHOTS OF YOUR PETS, A SOCK PUPPET OR AN AVATAR. (You'd be surprised.)

CHANGING THE PHOTO EVERY MONTH. This shows indecision and insecurity. Keep a photo up for long periods of time so people can learn who you are.

SPECIAL EFFECTS. Save the sepia tones and the GIF files for your Facebook page. Maybe someday they might be ubiquitous but for now just start with a basic shot.

Now please hear me: You do not have to hire a professional to get this photo done! I know many people pay a lot of money to have photos done and if you have a lot of money and want to do that it definitely can be nice. But for those of you who only have a cell phone camera and a friend, you are just fine. Take a photo and put it up. If you hate it, you can change it once, just don't keep changing it. Most photos taken by a friend should be easily uploaded to LinkedIn, but there are technological specifications to look into if you have something larger or in an unusual format.

Your LinkedIn picture can be as large as 4MB in size and can be in the following file formats: GIF, JPG, and PNG. It must also be within the maximum limit of 4000 x 4000 pixels. To upload a photo to LinkedIn, simply go to your profile page and click on the space where your photo would be that says 'Edit Photo'.

These days' images carry quite a bit of power online so harness that power with a photo of you that dazzles or at least represents you well. If potential employers see your photo, your image should prompt them to click on your profile to learn more about you. Does a cover represent the book? Certainly not in reality, but in a job search you need every bit of leverage you have. So create that proper 'cover' look that will encourage future employers to open your profile and read more about you.

RECOMMENDED

RECOMMEND ME, PLEASE!

We all know the importance of connecting with others when looking for work. It's the single most important thing to do and some, if not all, of today's business-social tools make it easier, but you have to understand how to use them.

Let's stick with Linkedin.com as our example. Linking to others on LinkedIn is really easy. If you look for and 'link' to people you know, you will quickly see other possible people to link with, generated automatically by the software itself much like it does on other social networks such as Facebook. In this case 'linking' is the same as 'connecting', meaning if you connect on the site you can see that person's profile and connections. This site is heavily focused on making connections and profiles are professional in nature as opposed to Facebook where things are usually more personal.

LinkedIn is free to use up to a certain point and you can expect to connect to your friends without paying, but if you want to dig in and use the site more intensely to make business connections, then there are pay walls set up to allow for extras, such as being able to message a stranger.

There are many people at all levels of business on LinkedIn, from baseball coaches to C-class executives. It serves many purposes and you are going to benefit from joining even if you have no intention of writing to anyone on the site. First of all, if you work in human resources you probably already use the site to seek professionals you need or review people who apply for work. Secondly, if you're looking to find out who it is you need to know to get a foot in the door, this site can show you numerous people in the same company and their related positions. So without making even one connection or link, you gain valuable information.

I do suggest you reach out to colleagues you know and send an invite to link up. When you see a (+) CONNECT button it means you can link or connect to that person. When you click on that button it will open to a box that says, 'I'd like to add you to my professional network on LinkedIn.' But I suggest adding one short line that says something more personal about why you want to link. If it's a friend or colleague you know, it won't matter much as they will probably just accept your connection. But if it's someone you only met once or maybe someone you have never met, then you should say something relevant; however, be brief.

There are two philosophies about making 'friends' online and only you know what's best for you. Some people only want to connect to people they know, others want to reach out to others. Make connections with anyone you want; there are no rules other than those driven by your own personal tastes.

You will also see a section for recommendations on your profile. I suggest you get a recommendation or two, especially if you see and link up with past colleagues on the site. Requesting a recommendation on LinkedIn is easy, just go to your profile, click 'edit' and then scroll down to recommendations. Click on the little pencil icon and you will see a link saying, 'ask for recommendations', or go to 'settings' on the right hand side and then, 'manage recommendations' on your settings page. The technology makes asking for a recommendation online easier these days, but in general this is not something you should take lightly. We could dedicate an entire piece to the subject of business recommendations and it might not be enough to emphasize its relative importance.

In this case get right to the point - its part of the nature of the site. The site will automatically generate a note to send and it usually says:

'I'm sending this to ask you for a brief recommendation of my work that I can include in my LinkedIn profile. If you have any questions, let me know. Thanks in advance for helping me out.'

You can certainly use that but if you want to stand out even a little, try something original, maybe something to the effect of:

'Dear _____,

I enjoyed working with you on the _____ project and was wondering if you might take a moment to recommend me on this site. I appreciate your contribution to my profile, thank you.'

We all know that whether you're a job seeker or a business owner, there is no single more powerful tool for furthering your ambitions than a well-timed, glowing and sincere recommendation. Word of mouth is always the best marketing, even in self-marketing, and if it comes from someone considered to be a 'trusted source' then your chances of success will go through the roof.

Getting that recommendation in writing is something you should also follow up with after the person writes you a LinkedIn recommendation. There are times when you need a written recommendation and if the person has already said yes to writing one, it won't be hard to transfer that to a sheet of stationery. You can copy and paste the recommendation from LinkedIn to a Word document and send it back to them for it to be placed onto stationery. Make it easy for people and they will help! Still nervous about asking for one? Don't be. Start here: impress people. It's generally good practice and you will be surprised at how it reverberates throughout your career. And it's never too late to start.

For a business recommendation for LinkedIn you can also follow these basic rules to be more successful in getting good recommendations:

CONTACT PEOPLE YOU KNOW. Although you may 'friend' anyone, you should only ask for recommendations from people you know.

MAKE IT EASY FOR THEM! Offer to write a sample that they can customize; include specifics you may want mentioned and remind them of something you did and its outstanding result. Don't expect others to remember everything about you.

EMAIL OR CALL THE PERSON ALONG WITH SENDING THE LINKEDIN REQUEST. Tell them that you sent the request and that you really appreciate their consideration.

TELL THE PERSON WHY YOU ARE ASKING. It gives you a chance to let this person know how much you respect him or her.

Offer to return the favor.

Try to get three recommendations. The truth is without any you might be fine and with seven or eight you might do really well. Don't fret over it. Three is a fair amount. Those that have thirty or more recommendations on LinkedIn, I tend to think of as people who overcompensate, but maybe that's just me.

If you can, get a list of people you want recommendations from and go about it right, contacting them beforehand and making it easy for them. Ask them if you can use this recommendation in any form and let them know if someone might be contacting them. If you can, explain to them beforehand that you will send a message through LinkedIn that they can easily respond to. When you get the recommendation look for one sentence you can pull out and use in a conversation. This way you can have quotes available when in an interview someone asks what your past employer might say about you - and it will sound authoritative. Plus you will know exactly what people will say about you if called upon later on for a referral.

Everyone loves a good recommendation. It reminds us of how much we are appreciated and how we actually do touch others lives. Give it that kind of thought when you ask for one. Give others recommendations that are fair and helpful if so deserving. I highly recommend it.

FINDING THAT OPPORTUNITY

There is no one best way to find a job opportunity. But there is a best way to notice opportunity. Here's my version of how it works.

Have you ever sat back and wondered how some people saw the Internet coming and created mega-fortunes building websites? Or how some people saw ways to capitalize on the Wall Street booms of the 90's? Or others who might have even started a modest business a decade ago and who now have small companies? What do these people all have that you need? Believe it or not it's rarely about others seeing opportunities that you don't. We all knew at a certain point that the web was going to be huge. What they see to a better degree than most is that **any action taken is infinitely more powerful than doing nothing**.

SPOTTING LEADS. A lead can come from anywhere, which is why if you're looking for a job, you never really stop working. There are ways to be a bit like Sherlock Holmes in your search and hopefully here we can outline some of those strategies for you. Keep in mind, though, that none of the following may ultimately help you find your next job because it often comes from someplace least expected, which is why doing literally anything helps you at all times.

Most people think of leads in terms of friends they have who are well connected. That's a great place to start, but try to look at opportunity differently, in other words, **see needs as leads**. What do we mean by that? We mean look around you and see what needs to be done. What do people around you need? When you spot something that aligns with your skill set, you now have a legitimate reason to approach someone and offer your help. This is how you can develop leads beyond your address book.

Think of things without the thick history of your past. If you think finding a job is pure drudgery and a negative experience then it already sets you off course. Is it drudgery? Of course it is! But if you start looking around, seeing the world as a place with a ton of things that need be done, then you may stumble upon someone willing to pay you to actually do it. So look for needs and turn them into leads.

You need a positive reason to be relentless. It's awfully hard to be relentless if you *kinda-sorta-not-really-somewhat* want that position at the publishing company. Start to see 'jobs' as opportunities to get things done and not always so rigidly defined as some set of duties and obligations.

As for traditional leads, you must also keep up with your meetings. Let's look at some of the basic ways in which you can increase your chances of finding "people" leads:

NETWORKING – This is the single most powerful tool in your search for anything, so get really good at it or fake it if you have to! For those who think networking is too difficult, think again. Start with those closest to you, your friends and family. Remember – if you don't ask you won't know and you will be left out. Ask for help from people when you need it and then REMIND people if they seem to forget. Always be polite and always write thank you notes. All these same rules from old school business still apply in the 'new world'; you just have more tools to do things with. You can use email to say thank you, just remember that a follow up in snail mail pushes you even further ahead.

If you feel like you don't know where to begin with your networking, then make a list of people you admire and write letters seeking their advice. It's not going to move every single person to want to help you, but if you get one response in ten you made it worthwhile. And asking for advice is always a great way to open a dialogue. In general try to be around people as much as possible, but be sincere in your efforts or it will not be as effective.

TRADE GROUPS/AFFILIATIONS – Each industry has groups and trade organizations so if you're thinking of going into a certain area of business or particular industry, then you must find these groups. What better way to do so but to attend some meetings? It's always better to find people with like-minded interests rather than join a group just because the people are `important`. However, let's be smart here; if you have the chance to be around influential people at an event or a party then by all means, do so! I think the key to networking is finding that perfect balance between being aggressive and not being desperate. Being yourself is always going to work best, but if you tend to not ask or not initiate conversations, you will have to push yourself a little. And don't get discouraged - about any of this. If you have a hard time talking to people at an event, try harder next time. Just go. And once at an event, start networking; don't wait until the event is half over like many people do!

COLLEGE/SCHOOL ALUMNI – Depending on where you went to school and how long ago you graduated, this resource can be extremely valuable. Talking with fellow alumni often leads to insider information when it comes to job openings and a referral from fellow alumni can be powerful. Check back with your alumni office. There are usually outlets in every major city and with the Internet (the 'new world' in action!) you can connect with people you may have lost touch with from around the world.

JOB FAIRS – Companies often send employee recruiters to job fairs and though these can leave you feeling a bit like a lost sheep if you've not been to one, there is great value in attending the better ones. Stick to ones you know that specialize in your areas of interest and always check to see who is attending.

HEADHUNTERS – For those seeking some of the higher-level executive jobs, utilizing the services of a professional recruiter or headhunter is the best way to go. They have the inside track on what employers are looking for and often can act as a sort of matchmaker. If you find yourself needing a headhunter, then you probably have peers who know someone, so ask around. And remember to never pay an application fee if someone asks you to do so. Maybe there is a legitimate reason for one somewhere out there, but in almost all occasions it's a scam.

Seeing opportunity is one important part of finding your new career path, but what works even better than close examination is good old fashioned showing up.

CATCHING YOUR RIDE

The typical job search has evolved as fast as the average workplace and in some ways the advantages are on the side of the seeker - if the seeker knows what to look for. Though there are two truths about the search that do stand as constants, the first being yes, it really is who you know, and two, it's who you know.

Don't know anyone? Don't worry. What I mean by 'it's who you know' is that 80% of jobs ARE NEVER POSTED. That's a whole lot of jobs, and these are usually the better jobs in terms of pay and working terms. Think about it, you work at a bakery and the baker leaves. The owner says to everyone, 'if you know anyone send them in...' Or the owner goes to a bakery he already likes and tries to persuade another baker to come. The last thing the owner does is post the job on an Internet board. So if you are already in his circles, you have a much better chance. However if you're not, you need to know how best to use the jobs boards and where to find what you're looking for.

Before we dig into the topic of job boards and how to approach them, let's look at our total approach to an online job search. Thankfully it's not all that hard nowadays to get your resume in front of employers, but getting a job still remains as difficult as ever and that's our goal, right? Well everyone has a website these days so studying them and finding out who is who is important. It also makes available some email addresses so you can contact people directly. But a warning about this: do not contact someone directly unless you know what you are asking for.

WHAT'S OLD IS NEW AGAIN.

Remember those old job listings in newspapers? Uh, no, me neither, but I have heard of them--the rows of repetitive ads for people that fit a title within an industry offering a contact number to send a resume through the mail. Well today this process has of course been supplanted by an online version, and if you look closely it can both help and hurt your chances of finding that perfect job.

A FEW THINGS TO KNOW ABOUT JOB BOARDS ONLINE: Everyone now has access. Yes, everyone has access! That was true even when these jobs were listed in a local newspaper's classified section. With the ease of posting a job now being advantageous to the employer, sometimes employers will post jobs just to see what resumes come in, even when they aren't actively looking to fill the position. (It's sometimes why you see postings remain on job boards for long periods of time.)

The online job board world is a network of sites and message centers that enable employers to connect with job seekers much in the same way as online dating sites if you think of it that way; by using algorithms to match certain key indicators like salary, location and title, they can show you what jobs are posted seeking people much like yourself. (Algorithm is just a fancy word for secret computerized formulas that crank out answers based on what you input.)

Here are some other things you need to know about job boards:

HEY GET YOUR JOBS HERE!

Unfortunately it's not really that easy. Many of the sites will ask you to sign in using your email. This is common practice and might even be good for those who want to receive email alerts about possible job matches. Just remember to use an email that is professional if you're applying and write down all of your passwords somewhere because you will have a lot of them.

READ CAREFULLY. Any site that asks for payment upfront without a trial period should be looked at carefully. Yes, some sites like TheLadders.com are legitimate and helpful sites, and I know a few that are pay-only sites, but in general do not pay for job search results. There are too many free ones out there to try first and usually the employer pays any upfront fees on those.

You will notice many of the job sites will take you to another employer-based site calling for yet another sign in process. Although ridiculously time-consuming and redundant, this is not a scam and for many larger corporations it's basic protocol, so have patience.

Have a PDF version of your resume ready to send, and open on your desktop for attaching to emails. I say keep one open so that you can slightly customize each if you need to. If you're not sure how to make a PDF out of that Word or other text document simply go to `file' and hit `save as' and it should offer you the option to save your resume as a PDF version.

Once you get to searching for jobs, you can quickly become lost in a maze. On each site, you will want to refine your search. Trying different modifiers will help until you get the idea.

Here's what I call a "Street Tip" because it's off-the-record-unofficial and, in reality, unproven other than by myself and my friends:

STREET TIP! Obviously you want to enter your location and your job title as parameters in a search, but maybe start with a wider net and then make it smaller. That will allow you to see at what point things like salary and job descriptions change. If you are a graphic designer, first start with a search that includes `art director' and see what results come up. Besides seeing how this position is different from yours, notice something important: if a company is hiring a position above you, there is a good chance that after that person is hired, he or she will want to bring in new people. So if you see an opening `above' you, make a mental note and in a month send a resume and a nice cover letter.

Next up is the resource list of job sites and we'll give tips for how to best use them in your search. Remember that these sites have slightly different ways of working but some general basics apply so once you get the hang of it, you really can move quickly through numerous postings at a time. Sites designed for people in your industry, niche, or job title will often yield higher percentage results so a good strategy is to begin on these sites and work outward to the more general sites. On the other hand, larger sites can offer a better overall look at what the landscape looks like so if you have time for research, look at those to get a take on what's going on. You ultimately will want to use all of them, but do so systematically or this job search can turn into a full time, non-profit job itself.

FIND YOUR DREAM JOB

t is my hope at this point that we all have a decent bird's eye view of the current hiring landscape, even as it changes and evolves almost every month. We have gone from job classifieds in newspapers to a world in which companies at every level are utilizing the Internet to find many of their new hires. But at the same time it's still about making connections and drawing upon relationships so things aren't all that different in some ways.

As with all things, along with the advantages come the disadvantages and now that companies and even small businesses have gone to online job postings to find those new people, understand that this means employers also have more control over who sees these job postings simply by where they choose to post them and how they choose to filter them.

Today's job applicants send their resumes through what can be a maze of software doors, each only allowing for speedy passage if it meets certain specific guidelines. The first thing is to make sure that the title of your last job matches or is closely related to the posted job title. Software programs can filter resumes using this input alone.

Like true love, a great job can and usually does emerge from a busy life filled with meeting people, instead of being 'discovered', as is the usual belief about good jobs. And great jobs are not always so great in and of themselves - that is until someone gets into the position and steers it to its full potential. So keep this same openness of mind when you hit the job boards online because these job boards are not enough to use alone; you must keep networking at all times.

The job boards can seem a lot like high powered classifieds and they are, but they also can be littered with fake postings, spam, and even scams that are easy to avoid if you know some basic rules. When you search always have your resume ready and open a search engine to look up each company you apply to. Send your resume freely but to be safe, minimizing spam and avoiding common scams, let's touch on a few thoughts:

Take your exact mailing address off of your resume, save for the city and state, just as I advised in your email signature. In today's new world, all that an employer needs to contact you are your name, phone number, email address, and then city and state for reference. So at the top of your resume, your mailing address should go from this:

Mary Johnson
105 East 105 Street Apt. 4G
Brooklyn, NY 11236
646-345-9876
maryjohnson@gmail.com

To this:

Mary Johnson
New York, NY 11236
646-345-9876
maryjohnson@gmail.com

Always send a PDF or JPG, never a WORD document to an employer, unless specified to do so. PDF's are the most commonly used format and it is essentially a locked document that cannot be changed. This helps dissuade anyone with any unkind ideas from easily copying and pasting your contact info into a document and saving it for something other than your job search.

Using a PDF won't stop everyone from using your information but it is harder to copy and paste something from your resume or to change a PDF document so they might be likely to move on to the next one. It's kind of like having a loud barking dog in your house that does next to nothing – but it might send the bad guys elsewhere. Just note as you read this I am being cautious here - I don't think problems are extremely common but as this process grows and more data is stored by everyone I think it's wise to start looking at security as part of this process.

HERE'S A BIG ONE. Never, ever give your Social Security number out to anyone you do not know and this would include all of your potential employers in an online application. If the electronic application asks for it, leave it blank. If you're applying for that dream job at the most prestigious firm ever then I would simply pick up the phone and verify that the site you are about to send your Social Security number to is actually the site before just sending it. The reality is that they shouldn't even be asking for it until you meet face to face.

So here we go. Turn off the news reports and think positive. Here is a list of job boards to start. This list is a resource that you can return to every day you search. Some of these are major job boards that show as many jobs as possible, some are more targeted towards a niche, and some are simply support systems for people looking.

THE JOB BOARD RESOURCE LIST

MONSTER Very large, a good site to look at but many higher level position-seekers feel its time has passed.

CAREERBUILDER Similar to Monster – both are good places to set up and gather alerts for those positions that match your skill set.

INDEED A good place to start. It's easy and pulls from many sites on this list so it might be one of the best here.

SIMPLYHIRED This site is very similar to Indeed, but with half the monthly traffic.

AOL Believe it or not AOL is seen as something from "the olden days" to anyone 40 and under.

SNAGAJOB Primarily a niche site used by employers of hourly workforces.

USAJOBS This site created by the federal government is great for veterans and boasts a nice resource center.

JOB.COM A site for general job seekers, though I think it owes much of its success to owning a great domain name.

THELADDERS When it launched it only listed jobs paying $100K or more but since 2011 has lowered that bar. Still it attracts higher level positions – and is one of the few that asks for payment from both employers and job seekers.

DICE This is a great site for technology professionals, but if you are one, you probably already knew this.

FINDTHERIGHTJOB I've never been crazy about a site that makes you sign in just to see job postings.

JOBBANK USA Not a well made site but it does have lots of listings if you click "Multi Database Listings".

JOBSTER An up-and-comer with nice features, definitely worth a look.

LINKUP Great site because it also crawls corporate sites for jobs.

LINKEDIN As we know from a past chapter, this site is helpful in many ways. Check out their job listings as well.

VAULT Also from a past column, this site is useful as a resource for all things work-related.

RILEY GUIDE A lesser-known resource this is a site that divides job boards according to industry.

MEDIABISTRO For media-related jobs this is it.

MASHABLE For tech and media-related jobs this is also it.

CRAIGSLIST Obviously not always a trusted source, it can be incredibly helpful for people seeking entry-level positions.

IDEALIST For those socially conscious job seekers, try this site.

TWEETMYJOBS A new player on the scene, this site and others like it will become more prominent as job seeking takes a social twist.

SMARTBRIEF An industry-specific and highly informative resource.

HEAD FOR COVER

O f all the things you need to get a job, the one that in many cases is the most debated, revised and strategized over may be the cover letter. The resume tells a lot about you, but the cover letter tells them more. Just ask the people who read them. I did and after talking to those hiring managers, I am convinced that a great resume may get you an interview but a well-written cover letter could get you a job. What do I mean by that? Let's see.

Hiring managers routinely scan resumes first and then read cover letters because if you don't have the training or background it won't matter, you won't get an interview, but if you do have the right resume, well suddenly that cover letter is the BEGINNING of your interview. So a well written one can make a huge difference in the part of your job search that will become crucial - what a sales team might call the conversion (actually getting the job).

COVER ALL BASES. Writing a successful cover letter is perhaps the most difficult part of the application process and obviously we could talk at length on the best way to construct a cover letter from scratch but the amount of variables involved when talking in generalities is too large to make sense of it all, so let's focus on a particular type: a short cover email that you use to apply to online jobs such as those posted on the job boards. There are many ways in which this differs from a hard copy format so for the moment don't try and adapt your actual cover letters to a cover email, if only because you will form bad habits that are harder to break later, so start fresh.

Remember that these hiring managers are in most cases seeing literally hundreds of emails so rule number one is keep it short and to the point.

DIVIDE AND CONQUER. I suggest breaking it into three small parts: 1) the introductory section, 2) the 'why you think you're right' section and 3) the 'thank you and contact me section.' When I say 'section' I mean one or two sentences tops.

And something all of the hiring managers I talked with said was to always address your emails or letters to a specific person rather than 'To whom it may concern' which works if no names are provided

STREET TIP! Try using www.Hoovers.com to find out the person you should write to. This site lists lots of businesses.

Here is a basic email cover sample one would send with a resume attached:

> *Dear Mrs. Smith,*
>
> *I am submitting my resume for consideration for the position of beekeeper.*
>
> *My unique skills as a professional beekeeper have helped me to win various awards from Ohio all the way to Florida, and I have never been stung.*
>
> *I have attached my resume along with some sample images of my honey. Please contact me at this email or at 001-555-1234 to set up a meeting at your convenience.*
>
> *Sincerely,*
> *You*

I wrote this with a (perhaps failed) attempt at humor hoping that no one actually copies this for use, because that is a temptation for many job seekers At least half of the job applicants I spoke with admitted taking a sample directly from the web. There's merit in borrowing ideas from others, but if you don't personalize your message you are losing a huge opportunity. Instead of being overly formal see this as a chance to be brief and informative yet enticing the reader to call you in because of something you offer.

Lastly you want to make sure to customize each email cover to match the job posting. This isn't as hard as it sounds. Make sure the addressee is different, so you don't send an email to the wrong person. The official's title should read as it is posted. Then include one or two lines usually near the end of the email that show that you didn't just copy and paste the salutation mindlessly. Say something specific that will separate you from the rest but keep it professional and pertinent to the job description.

SAMPLES PLEASE. If you are looking for highly specialized jobs such as graphic designer, architect, copywriter or a job that specifically requests work samples, then take your best work and make them into PDF's as we did for your resume. When sending samples, a general rule of thumb is to send less but send high quality, rather than sending an overwhelming package of work. If you already have samples you probably know how best to create them for use as needed in your line of work, but if needed turn to peers or industry specific blogs for ways in which to put your samples in the best presentation possible.

Now let's get ready because it's about that time. That's right, it's time for you to reach out and impress someone. All of these tools you are developing are designed to get you motivated and out there because only then will you find that job in the new world. You must look at the application package and especially the cover letter as preludes to an interview, a way of introducing yourself just before you walk through that door.

Once you start sending out your resume you are going to want to keep track of these emails by either labeling them or stashing them in a folder in your email portal. Make sure to do this because when someone calls you they might not always respond to the email directly and you will want to know to whom you are speaking.

Here's your next assignment: pick out an interview outfit and visualize yourself sitting in a chair in that outfit impressing the heck out of someone who is looking for a great employee. Do this three times a day until you read the next chapter and you will be more ready for that interview than ever.

CALL WAITING

All set for that job interview? Of course you are. By now you've gone over your shtick a few times, you have your outfit and resumes ready, and you have practically mastered the firm handshake.

But before anything happens you may have to manage some careful correspondence, more specifically emails from potential employers.

The first thing I am sure you all are wondering is, 'Why is he spending so much time talking about how to respond to an email? We all know how to do that.' Bear with me. Some of you may see my comments as a refresher course, but how to respond to an email from a potential employer is not as simple as it sounds. What works today may not work tomorrow, so it's best to be vigilant about current trends. Do your homework and it won't hurt to pause before you hit that 'send' button.

After that email has been sent, and then you wait, right? How long should you wait before contacting the person again? A week, two weeks, a month? Again, there's no one right answer. Much will depend upon the position and what you have read online, and in other places, about the company's hiring practices. Here are three things to consider:

1. Some HR managers cannot stand being contacted and will think you are 'high maintenance'. Is it right? No. But possession is 9/10ths the law and they have what you want so honor their thoughts on the matter.

2. Chose the right way to communicate. Email is a good way to check in. Calling is not something I recommend unless you are terrific at cold calling and can phrase your approach so as not to appear annoying or pushy. Good old snail mail is actually the best way to ask for an update. A written note gets attention.

3. No matter how you approach the hiring manager, be polite. Remember to be brief and say thanks.

If you know something about a situation not covered here, then go ahead and break all the rules. These are general guideposts worthy of attention, but there's a fine line between being smart about something and over-thinking it, so if you feel strongly about veering off the general consensus then go right ahead. Sometimes the aggressive approach is rewarded. Go with your instincts because often these can help separate you from the crowd. On the other hand, I would not suggest sending more than one follow up email or making more than one call unless otherwise told to do so.

There are many systems that generate 'an auto response' where you are told your resume has been received. Don't get too excited, this usually means little besides your resume making it through the maze of technology to someone's inbox.

Then there is the possibility that you will receive an email from the HR department or someone else from the company. Now you are getting somewhere! You might be asked to clarify something from your resume or schedule a time for a phone interview. Now you're talking. Please resist the temptation to shoot off a response from your cell phone unless you type well. I have follow-up mails from phones that are filled with spelling mistakes which does not set a good tone.

The email you want to respond with isn't difficult to write. Just don't spell names or anything else wrong. You've already impressed them so keep it simple, and try something like this:

Dear Ms. Cunningham,

Thank you for taking the time to review my resume.
I will be available to take your call today/tomorrow at any time
between 1-5 p.m.

You may reach me at 212-555-1234 at anytime/state time
available.

Sincerely,
You

A word about these emails: sometimes there are fakes and scams out there. If you fill out enough applications online you eventually will see some of these fake postings that are too repetitive to be real, but for now just be aware of them. It's part of the process and, unfortunately, there's really no way to avoid being a target. Here are the signs that something about a potential employer's response is fishy:

If you see an unusually long response, three or more paragraphs, be wary. A potential employer is not going to take the time to write paragraphs to you. If it makes no reference to anything from your resume, it's certainly spam, so don't answer it.

If it tells you that there is a 'main office in the UK or Europe' and this will be their attempt to 'establish a location in the U.S.,' then beware. This is a common scam where they would ask you to open a bank account in the states.

Rule number one - DON'T ANSWER IT. Now that I said that I still will follow with this: If it asks you to give them your name, address and Social Security number and...yes that's right I said your Social Security NUMBER, then please DON'T ANSWER IT. If there is no phone number to call any-where to be seen then ...DON'T...well you get the idea. Click spam imme-diately and delete it from your computer. This type of spam won't hurt your computer but never respond to it. As I said before, never give out your Social Security number in an online job application.

OK, so back to our search. You sent the resume and actually received an email setting up an interview or a phone call or perhaps - both. Hopefully, during that phone call, you will be asked to come in and meet someone from HR, but just as likely these days you may have to do a mini-interview over the phone first. In the next chapter we will sharpen our phone interview skills just in case.

TELL A PHONE TO HIRE YOU

ere's something new about the current workplace: depending upon your industry as many as one in six job interviews now begins on the phone. This is an additional step in the process we are all used to, a phone interview acting as a gatekeeper for the HR department before they let you in for an interview. Companies looking to save time and money choose to pre-screen applicants on the telephone rather than with a face-to-face meeting. How this affects you is important.

For some, this development is good news. Imagine sitting at home in sweat-pants and flip-flops, drinking coffee from a favorite mug, and still interviewing for that dream job. You may find this part of the new process relaxing; you can have your notes out and ready and you don't have to be judged by your appearance and age.

Other applicants who do much better in an actual meeting may regard this trend as a lost opportunity; it's not and here's why. Many HR managers tell me that they use this tool to include people in the process they might not have called before. This doesn't mean you are one of those people, it just means you are the beneficiary of a new system that has a wider gate.

No matter your point of view, the phone interview may be a necessary step in your job search. See it as your chance to shine so that even before the conversation is over, you will be assured of winning that in-person interview. Yes, you can lay the foundation for a good interview in a phone interview even if you dislike it.

My advice? Prepare for that phone interview as you would for an actual interview – because it is! The goal here is two-fold: to impress the interviewer with who you are, and to get that face-to-face interview. Do your homework. Learn about the company, the people, and the position you are applying for and have a look at the website. In the days of search engines like Google and Bing, employers think it insulting not to know the basics.

Ask yourself some basic questions and have answers ready. In most cases the employer will tell you what the call is about. What strengths will you bring to the job and to the company?

You obviously won't have to worry about what to wear or bring to the interview, but there are important ways to prepare:

» **IF YOU CAN, ALWAYS USE A LANDLINE.** If you don't have access to one, then charge your cell phone or plug it in as you talk. No Bluetooths and no speaker phones. And yes, it's a bad thing if your phone drops the call so get to a spot you know has a good connection.

» **OPEN UP THE COMPANY WEBSITE ON YOUR COMPUTER AS YOU TALK TO THEM.** You want to be focused on what they are saying, but when on the phone one's eyes tend to wander. This way your eyes will wander where it may help.

» **GET SOME WATER READY.** You may get a dry mouth when you are talking for a length of time. Obviously never eat while on the phone. (Do I have to say that?)

» **GET YOUR RESUME OUT, YOUR COVER LETTER, ANY NOTES, AND ANY**

CORRESPONDENCES ALONG WITH BLANK PIECES OF PAPER AND TWO PENS. Yes, two pens; you know one always runs out. Have all of it ready because they might ask you about that project manager position at Sunbeam in 1992 and you want to sound consistent with what you sent to them.

» **TELL ANYONE IN THE HOUSE OR LOCATION NOT TO WALK IN OR DISTURB YOU.** This one surprisingly evades many people because they think the interviewee will understand. And yes in many cases they will, but what is it saying about you as a first impression? See what I'm saying? So to increase every advantage keep people and pets out of barking distance.

Now comes the hard part. The call. Relax and be yourself. I know everyone says that but what does it mean? It means being honest. If you come off as a 'hard sell' on the phone people generally get turned off more so than if you do it in person.

Don't under sell yourself or be meek. Be forceful in your answers, but also know when to be light and avoid sounding robotic. One easy way to do this is to stay focused and listen. Listening is a skill and as important to an interviewer as speaking, if not more so.

Here's the deal - that person on the other end of the phone probably has ten to fifteen interviews he or she will have to do, learning about you with every sweep of the second hand. If that person on the phone feels you are consistently interrupting them, or not paying close enough attention, or if you sound like your answers are too rehearsed, you are less likely to make it to the next round.

STREET TIP: If after rehearsing several times, you still feel nervous and unsure, think about finding a coach. Many former HR people now work as job coaches and you may benefit not only from their help with the interview but with their insight on the entire hiring process.

When you speak, speak with confidence and be the 'you' people like work-ing with. Visualize yourself sitting in their office. Keep in mind you might even be on speaker phone with other team members listening in, but do not acknowledge that unless told so.

It does help to be conversational during this phase even when talking about your accomplishments. Most of all - be positive. You may find that you actu-ally enjoy speaking to the person on the other end of the line and if that hap-pens, you have the most chance of success.

Before you hang up, make sure you have the interviewer's contact informa-tion so that you can send a 'thank you' as a follow-up. Now you should feel dialed in.

21

DRESS & REHEARSAL

You have arrived. You got the call, you flew through the phone interview, and now they want to meet you. It's time for the interview.

I want to make sure that we emphasize the importance of the interview by taking two sections to cover it, dividing this opportunity into the 'pre-interview' phase and then 'the interview.' The interview will decide whether you get the job because people hire people and not resumes, so take your time when preparing for this meeting.

In the 'pre-interview' phase we could say there are two main areas to address, the mental and the physical.

First let's address the physical aspects which include not only your general appearance and outfit, but also your body language, handshakes and eye contact. Research tells us that as much as 85 percent of communication is non-verbal. Make a task list and start with these tips:

> » **KNOW THE COMPANY'S CULTURE AND STYLE EXPECTATIONS.** You don't have to spend a fortune to get a job but if there are ways to look the part then do so.

> » **PLAN OUT EXACTLY WHAT YOU WILL WEAR TWO DAYS BEFORE.** When in doubt, go with

something conservative unless you know otherwise. The key here is to set aside one or two 'interview outfits' that are always clean and pressed and ready to go.

» **ON COLORS—KNOW THE RULES BEFORE YOU BREAK THEM.** Navy blue is always a good choice and grays with a white shirt or blouse always looks professional. Wear strong colors like black and red as accents only to show your personality, but be reserved if at all in doubt.

» **FOR WOMEN WEAR CLOSED TOE SHOES AND PLAIN HOSIERY.** And for men, make sure your shoes are freshly shined.

Now this may sound like a chore but it pays dividends: have a friend interview you as a rehearsal. Write out or suggest some basic questions you know you might be asked and respond seriously. You might be surprised what comes out of this exercise.

Notice your body language and eye contact. Eye contact should be steady and not locked in an unblinking glare. Sit up straight and don't slouch, especially if the chair you are given is deep and easy to slouch in. Don't fidget. Breathing deeply is the best way to quickly relax and can change your entire presence. Practice a few times until you can sit straight and look the interviewer in the eye in a natural, confident way.

The other part of your preparation is mental. Prepare your mind to handle anything you might be asked about in that interview. Of course you don't want to over-rehearse anything but running through an answer once or twice will help you immeasurably once you're under the bright lights. Start by knowing answers to the most basic questions almost always asked during an interview such as:

"Tell me a little bit about you."

"Why do you want to work here?"

"Why did you leave your last job?"

"Do you have any questions for us?"

STREET TIP: Have one or two but keep it positive, extremely simple and related to a work aspect of the job – not a benefit. Focus on the management style of the company and ask how the position fits within it. You might find out a lot about the company asking about this.

Here is a checklist for further mental preparation:

Know your resume by heart.

Know all of your strengths and ONE or TWO of your weaknesses.

Know your life story.

Know how to summarize your life story.

Know how to summarize your life story using only the highlights.

Know the history of the company you're interviewing.

Know what the company has interests in and what kind of image and marketing it does if any.

Know what the company website and what all of its social media tools look like.

Know the job description.

Know the person or people interviewing you.

Feel like this is information overload? It is. Having this information will help you relax and if you relax you will be more yourself and if you're more yourself, you might get that job.

Want a shortcut to this way of thinking? Here's how. Whatever you are asked in an interview remember to emphasize three things:

YOU ARE HIGHLY MOTIVATED. This means you don't simply enjoy your work, you are driven by it. No need to pull the 'I'm a perfectionist' routine though because that comes off as portraying you as someone who may be difficult and unreasonable to work with. There is no perfection in today's New World.

YOU WORK WELL WITH OTHERS. This is always going to be a question in an interviewer's mind and though saying it means virtually nothing, it does show that you understand how important it is.

YOU ARE ADAPTABLE. In today's world, things change fast and if you are someone who needs to be doing the same thing for the next 25 years you need to re-think how you approach this. Nobody wants that anymore and the people who get hired are people who can adapt.

Now prepare a basic thank you letter, note or email simply to have it ready to fill in with details and send the moment you get home. Outline it as a reminder because trust me; it's the last thing you will want to do from scratch when you finish the interview.

22

WHO'S WHO, INC.

S o here you are ready for your big interview because you can express your best qualities and you look like a million bucks. You have even studied the bios of the people interviewing you and you feel as if you can go in to the interview and nail it.

You're ready, trust me. But if you have been on the interview conveyor belt for a while now or if you're one of those folks who like to delve deeper into a subject then taking a look at corporate structures and how they hire might be worthwhile. If nothing else it will give you a giant helping hand when you do get hired because knowing who is who in your company, who does what and how it all works is the fastest way to making friends.

Understanding Organizational Structure can be complicated but doesn't have to be for the job seeker in you. How an organization is structured dictates how communications and reporting relationships work. Since the 1970's there has been a general 'flattening' of corporate structure in America meaning that layers of communication are taken out so that people can work faster and more effectively. This structure actually mimics the way a small business works. Large and mid-size companies now see the lack of management layers as a desirable way in which to deal with both the modern worker, and the speed of business.

According to the National Bureau of Economic Research, the number of managers in a company who report directly to the CEO has increased from an average of four in 1986 to an average of seven today, but these are now divisional managers, not solely senior executives. In general, the CEO is now closer to the average employee than ever.

As a job seeker this kind of structure can help you in getting hired - that is if you understand how it works.

KNOW THE LINGO (you will hear me say this again trust me). It's OK to feel lost in a world of jargon when listening to a conversation between your 15-year old son and his friends concerning the best formats to download Internet music. But when it comes to a career you need to know what common words and phrases mean. It's impossible to keep up and no one would spurn your candidacy because you didn't know a technology acronym but if you don't know what a COO is or does, then you need to study.

Here is an easy overview that should get you started and is probably redundant for many. A corporate hierarchy is simply a structure where everyone reports to someone else - except for the owner or CEO who runs the show.

If you are dealing with a large corporation or public company (a public company is one that offers shares on Wall Street) you probably will see a Board of Directors. This is typically the top of the food chain. The Board Members are elected by shareholders and if you are interviewing for a position at a company with a Board, well, chances are you will never see or hear from them. However, if you go into an interview and don't know who they are, you risk looking uninformed should it come up. What's more, if there were someone on the Board who knew a colleague of yours, then you are losing an opportunity to network.

Beneath the Board are the Corporate Officers: CEO, CFO, COO, CMO and other assorted newcomers like CTO. If you know these five you are in good shape.

> **CEO**- Chief Executive Office

> **CFO**- Chief Financial Officer

» **COO** - Chief Operating Officer

» **CMO** - Chief Marketing Officer

» **CTO** - Chief Technology Officer

Different corporations use different hierarchies but generally underneath the Officers are Vice Presidents (VP) and then underneath them the Directors, underneath that layer are Managers and then underneath them are the inadequately described "average workers" or employees.

I can hear you now, "What the heck, Jason. I can learn all this when I get a job!" You're right you can. But here is why you shouldn't: the trend in the new American jobscape is to hire based on employee referrals. This means that companies are not just calling references or seeking resumes with big names but instead if someone working at any level in the company knows and likes you - it can translate to a hire.

Many job recruiters and hiring managers are now starting to see groupings of job seekers emerge. There are those that only seek positions through Internet sites and these are not appealing to most hiring managers. The ones who submit for positions in conjunction with employee referrals are actually part of a group of job seekers called 'purple squirrels' because of their rarity. But trust me - when a hiring manager sees a purple squirrel, they usually hire them.

So beyond knowing who is interviewing you, it can be valuable to know anyone in the company at all so it is worth your time to get online and find out who is working at any of the named positions above. You might be surprised. Find out you know the District Manager in another department? Make a call and see if s/he can help you.

Knowing that the flattening of the hierarchy means quicker access both up and down the ladder we also can see who makes the decisions and how best to address these people. For instance if you see a job opening for a Division Manager and you meet with a manager above you for the first interview it helps to understand that the Director or even VP above them might approve your hire.

Know who those people are and appeal to their needs. Did the VP attend the same university as you did? Does the Director have experience in the same expertise as you do? Knowing this information can lead to a more direct conversation and even help expedite the process.

So although you were already ready for the interview before this, snapping on your big purple bushy tail and hitting the web for more research might not be so nuts after all.

AT LAST, THE INTERVIEW

he first alarm goes off and just as you are about to hit snooze, a second, louder alarm goes off and it might be then that you remember me saying what a good idea it was to set two alarms the day of your big interview! Or maybe you want to throw your clocks at me.

Seriously it is rule number one to be on time. If you feel even the slightest bit rushed, you risk showing up looking frazzled. So set two alarms and tell your wife, husband, kids, someone to wake you. Get up, have your coffee, and stretch out a bit.

Having laid your clothes out the night before and with at least three copies of your resume in a nice folder or briefcase along with those same two working pens I told you to bring to the phone interview, you're ready to go. And of course you have the address and phone number of the interview location written down on a piece of paper, because the night before you went online and found directions to the company. Right?

As you make your way to the interview, stay relaxed and avoid cramming any last bits of information into your head, even things I have said. The time to get your game face on is before you leave the house not right before you enter the building. Be confident, smile at those you see along the way, and leave those voices of self-doubt at home. Let it be.

Remember something; the interviewer - at least nine times out of ten - WANTS you to be the right person. Think of it - they can finally stop searching and get to work if they find the right person. Searching for employees is an expense no company enjoys paying for.

OK RULES #1, 2 AND 3: ARRIVE EARLY. I cannot say this too many times. If you are late you will reduce to nearly zero your chances of even being considered for the job. Being late for an interview is always unacceptable – but it happens, so if it does, apologize to everyone once as you arrive and once as you leave. No more or less. After that you will need to blow them away with the interview itself, but don't keep mentioning your tardiness.

CHECK IN WITH THE RECEPTIONIST AND HERE ARE RULES #4AND 5: ALWAYS BE NICE TO THE RECEPTIONIST. Funny I should even have to say this but let's assume not everyone has the same sunny disposition. Then you should at least show some smarts because if you don't think that receptionists, assistants, doormen, and anyone else you might meet along the way don't help you in getting the job, then you haven't a clue. Receptionists I know often meet with their bosses after to discuss their impressions of you. Keep in mind a business owner isn't going to have someone sit at the front of the company whose opinion isn't valued.

When you walk through the door remember to feel confident that you are the right person for this job - because you are! Make certain to look people in the eye when conversing and when seated remember to be comfortable in the chair without slouching.

You say hello and after some small talk now come those questions we rehearsed. This will be a piece of cake, right? Of course. Be yourself when you answer, don't try and use big words just because you think it makes you sound intelligent or try to be funny if you don't feel it's genuine. But remember to be the best possible self you can be, which means be prepared, relaxed, and focused. Allow yourself to be enthusiastic about the opportunity, but always be sincere. Hiring managers are pretty good at sniffing out insincerity.

Another important point that I mentioned in my little story about phone interviews, is that your listening skills are a crucial component of what people think of you. Do you know how to truly listen? Are you anticipating what the person is going to say and are ready with an answer? Are you jumping in too quickly before taking even a breath? Staying calm will help all of this. This is why breathing deeply helps so much. If you can practice breathing exercises on a daily basis this will all be a bit easier. Make sure you are doing some nose breathing as well. Lastly try not to talk too fast because as we all have noticed when seeing others do it, it comes across as nervous and uncertain. Relax, relax, and relax. It keeps you looking confident but it also prevents you from anticipating answers and interrupting.

When the interview is coming to a close, make sure you have at least one question ready when they ask: 'Do you have any questions for us?' If you have other questions, you can add those, too, but remember to know the difference between a question and a concern. Don't bring up 'concerns' such as issues dealing with pay, vacation time, or holidays because you can always deal with these when an offer is made. For now keep questions pertinent to the position, the work and focus on getting the job. It's much better if you can show your insight into a position by asking a truly pointed question about the workflow, strategy or process involved.

When the interview is over thank everyone – and I mean everyone, including receptionists and doormen. Smile and shake hands when necessary and as soon as you get home fill out that thank you and send it off. Mention something particular about the process that you appreciated in the thank you message, and remember to thank the interviewer for his or her time.

Now make sure your phone is on at all times and start daydreaming about being employed there. Remember when I last spoke about daydreaming? Seems like an age ago now doesn't it? Good work.

OVERCOMING OBSTACLES AND REJECTION

The easy road leads nowhere. It's such a trite thing to say but it is something we are told as children and then somewhere along the line we seem to disbelieve it. Maybe things go your way a bit and you don't have a need to be 'easy road averse'.

Well the good news is that in a job search, many of us will not be taking the easy road, thus learning a lot from the experience, right?

Let's see here.

There will be a lot of rejection both upfront and a more painful type that happens after you interviewed four times and had dinner with your interviewer's family. It happens, and all the time. The cliché applies because it really is how you react - when the circumstances are within your control.

The key is to re-teach yourself what you can and cannot control because if you're anything like the rest of us, you lost clarity on this long ago.

As a quick reference point, you do not have control of many factors when it comes to looking for work. I do not include the excuse that 'it's the economy' because in every bad economy good industries rise and even when we are in a 'good economy' we hardly ever recognize it anyway. So yes, overall the economy is a factor, but then again so is the weather, right? You do not have control over the way an interviewer's morning went. You do not have control over the fact that the CEO's nephew is also a candidate. You do not have control over...well much of it. But that's OK. Because you don't need control - you need to be in the moment.

Let's say you walk in and shake the hiring manager's hand and then for the entire interview this person talks about his or her accomplishments and the company and barely asks you a thing. This happened to a friend who came to me after the interview saying the person was ridiculous for not asking her about her work and instead talked the whole time about himself and the company. How would the guy know if he should hire my friend? Why would he not ask her questions? Had he just staged this interview to talk about himself?

Of course he did! Because it isn't about you! If you don't understand that crucial point in this process then 'Houston, we have a problem'. Is it about both you and them in the grand scheme of things? Of course, it is! (I am not shouting I promise!) But during this phase of the relationship it's about them. There are far fewer people giving out jobs than taking them, it's just a fact. So it is about them and that's OK too.

It's OK because if you want to show them what you are TRULY about you will research and study your backside off and walk in there and even if you only say ten words they should be about something so insightful that only a good candidate would know it. And *bam* just like that you made it about you without them even knowing it.

The downside of all of these great technologies is that now you can be rejected more and faster than ever. So start to see obstacles and rejection beyond the painful experiences they are. Allow yourself ways to blow off steam because you might need to. Take a kickboxing class. Play tennis. Swim. It's frustrating even when it's going well. So give yourself a fighting chance. The way you come across in an interview or even in a cover letter can be traced to such subtleties you might never imagine. You need to seem happy, even if you're not! The good news is that action can create some happiness. Make someone smile and there's a good chance they will use you for something.

You can do some things to actively pursue handling rejection or as we shall now call them: opportunities. (Yeah, I went there.)

So how do I explain you sending a hundred resumes out and not getting one interview as an opportunity? Because aside from it being lousy, which it is, it does enable you to learn something that will change your circumstances and it might have to do with something as simple as your email address, your last job's title or that great idea you had one night to make a four color resume.

> » **SHOULD YOU SEARCH FOR REASONS THINGS DIDN'T WORK OUT?** No, look right in front of you. Be honest and clear about your goals and how realistic they are given your effort. Yes you stayed up all night working on it but that doesn't mean it's great - it's great when it's great so maybe you need to stay up two nights. Look for ways to improve, within reason of course.

> » **YOU SHOULD ALSO GIVE YOURSELF ONE THING TO ACCOMPLISH PER DAY** that you know you can. If it's a walk around the park or calling ten people it doesn't matter, as long as you can and do perform it.

> » **DO NOT GET AHEAD OF YOURSELF.** Two interviews in and you think the job is yours so you get lax on sending out thank yous to your other interviewers and then suddenly the job falls through and you're now behind and frustrated. No good. Always be working.

> » **DO SOMETHING ONCE A WEEK FOR NO REASON AT ALL.** Get away from all this nonsense for a bit. Fly a kite. Literally. Or go apple picking or watch all of Fellini's films in a row. Let go of expectations and see only the tasks in front of you. Do something whimsical - for you. In other words, shake things up a bit.

Take cold calling for instance. It's extremely frightening to some and yet if done in volume, can reap huge benefits. But hardly anyone does it? Why?

Because rejection is so awful to most of us that we'd rather not 'succeed' if it means being rejected along the way. Whoa! That's crazy, right?

No what's crazy is that nearly everyone whom you might consider successful would probably tell their story through the eyes of someone who was rejected. Over and over and over. So the real truth might be that there is no easy way to success.

By now you know I am not saying obstacles are always helpful. It's just that most times things we don't realize about ourselves are the things holding us back. Clear away some of those obstacles and you might be surprised at how things start to happen.

FROM DREAMS TO REALITY

Here you are. You have done a great job at interviewing for the job and now you sit by the phone and wait for it to ring, right? Wrong!

After impressing everyone at the interview you came home and sent a thank you note not just to the person interviewing you, but also to anyone who attended and sat in on the actual interview. Make sure to spell names correctly; it would be a shame to blow it now by accidentally turning a 'Mr.' into a 'Ms.'

Immediately after that, you need to turn your head toward positions elsewhere, not allowing yourself to become complacent but rather to use the success of this interview to buoy you to another. Doing begets doing.

Now that you went on one you might find it easier as you get more of these. So while you're feeling inspired keep looking and make sure you write down and address any difficulties that may have arisen in your last interview. Never get so hyped up about an interview that you're driving yourself nuts thinking it's the one and only way to your dreams - it isn't. It may be great and it may get you there, wherever *there* is, but you can always make it to your dreams by another means if for some reason you do not get the job. Remember this because you probably will be rejected more than once and it isn't personal.

As you begin to look into other options you may even hear the telephone ring with ...an offer! At first they might simply be requesting a second interview. This is quite good. It means you made the first cut and that is a difficult thing to do. Now you're in the running. In many industries this is a necessary step and you might even be asked to come back a third time. Remember that the same principles apply to each interview: be impressive and be consistent with anything you've said in past meetings.

Depending on your industry there may also be a background check and reference check. Best to contact references even if they know you are using their names, and alert them to any particulars from the previous interview so that they might be ready to answer specific questions.

When the process is over and an offer is made, take a few deep breaths before answering even if you already know what you want. Don't feel pressured to say yes on the spot. Tell the hiring manager how happy you are to hear from them and that you are certainly interested, but would like a chance to discuss this offer with your family. Believe it or not this actually makes you look like a more attractive candidate rather than yell "HOORAY WHEN DO I START!?"

We all know how easy it is to jump at the first offer when you need a job but look at the offer closely just to make sure you understand what the offer is and how it may suit you. Any business would rather you decline an offer that isn't right than accept the position only to leave soon after - so considering these aspects of the offer before your answer is prudent:

> » **MONEY** – Obviously this is one of the primary reasons for taking the job so make sure this job gives you enough to pay bills but also that the amount is enough to make you feel you are being paid what you're worth. If not, you will only have resentment later. Salary is a highly personal topic and you want to research average salaries online before accepting.

> » **BENEFITS** – Take a long look at the benefits package if there is one. Find out what amounts you are being asked to contribute and see how entering into family plans affect the package. Also ask when the benefits kick

in, which sometimes may be as long as ninety days. Other important considerations are vacation time and 401K contributions.

» **TRAVEL** – If it wasn't specifically enunciated during the interview they might present how much travel the position will involve. Make sure it is in line with your capabilities.

» **TRAINING** - What certifications will you need? Any career advancement requirements?

» **CULTURE** – What is the dress code? Are you expected to attend many social events? Are your religious holidays on their holiday calendar? Do some research before deciding how to respond to the offer.

» **GOALS** – Lastly take a look at how this position fits into your future career and life plans.

You may end up accepting or declining a job on the phone, but it also may be a good idea to follow up in writing to confirm the details. In this letter or email make certain to again thank them for the offer and state your decision clearly as well as the general terms of the agreement. Either way, make certain to be brief and grateful for the opportunity.

Next steps are ones you might be familiar with. You may be called in to meet with human resources or if it's a smaller company you might be called in to meet with supervisors. Orientations may take place and you might be asked to read corporate manuals. If there is training it should take place before the position starts and in almost all cases you are paid for this.

Congratulations. It's been a long hard road but you have done everything you can to put yourself in a position for success. Keep in mind this job is an opportunity to achieve your dreams and have an idea of how it fits into your overall life plan. Even if it isn't the ideal position you should take the attitude that you can turn this position into something more than it was intended to be.

With your new position and new dreams in place you are now well on your way to becoming all that you can be. You did it - but now the work really begins. Dream on!

ABOUT THE AUTHOR

Jason Veduccio is a writer and entrepreneur working across many fields using a combination of strategy, philosophy and humor to help increase productivity in people's lives and in their businesses. In his career, he has met with and interviewed hundreds of workers and job seekers to try and find out more about American workplace culture so that he could bring that valuable information to his clients. This is his first publication.

www.ingramcontent.com/pod-product-compliance
Lightning Source LLC
Chambersburg PA
CBHW060040210326
41520CB00009B/1201